Opposites Attract:
Magnetism

Steve Parker

Heinemann
LIBRARY

Chicago, Illinois

For information, address the publisher:
Heinemann Library, 100 N. LaSalle, Suite 1200, Chicago, IL 60602

Customer Service: 888-363-4266
Visit our website at www.heinemannlibrary.com

Printed and bound in China by South China Printing Company.
08 07 06 05 04
10 9 8 7 6 5 4 3 2 1

Library of Congress Cataloging-in-Publication Data

Parker, Steve.
  Opposites attract : magnetism / Steve Parker.
    p. cm. -- (Everyday science)
Summary: Describes what magnetism and magnetic fields are, how they work, and various ways that magnetism is used.
Includes bibliographical references and index.
  ISBN 1-4034-4815-9 (HC), 1-4034-6421-9 (PB)
  1. Magnetism--Juvenile literature. 2. Magnets--Juvenile literature.
[1. Magnetism. 2. Magnets.] I. Title. II. Everyday science (Heinemann Library (Firm))
  QC753.7.P37 2004
  538--dc22

                          2003014787

Acknowledgments
The publishers would like to thank the following for permission to reproduce photographs: Alamy/Goodshoot p.**5**; Corbis pp.**22**, **44**; Corbis/Noboru p.**16**, Corbis/ Bettman p.**19** Drew Super Photography/ Photographersdirect.com p.**6**; FLPA/Minden Pictures/Mike Parry p.**26**; Fraser Photos pp.**4**, **33**; Getty p.**52**; Getty/BrandX Pictures p.**30**; Harcourt Education p.**7**; Harcourt Index p.**51**; Photographers Direct p.**17** Tzaud Photo; Robert Harding p.**23**, Robert Harding/Brouard p.**35**; SPL p.**48**, SPL p.**8**/ Megna, SPL/Tek Image p.**9**, SPL/Volker Steger p.**13**, SPL/Professor Brian Wilshire p.**14**, SPL/Bluestone p.**15**, SPL/ Sinclair Stammers p.**18**, SPL/NASA p.**27**, SPL/Bartel p.**28**, SPL/Stock p.**36**, SPL/Siu p.**42**, SPL/Nunuk p.**46**, SPL/Tompkinson p.**49**; Trip p.**45** .High Field Magnet laboratory, University of Nijmegen, Netherlands p.**50**.

Cover photograph of the *aurora borealis* reproduced by permission of Robert Harding.

Artwork: Art Construction pp.**13**, **47**; Ascenders p.**34**; Mark Franklin pp.**20**, **25**, **29**, **39**, **40**, **43**; Visual Image p.**11**.

The publishers would like to thank Robert Snedden for his assistance in the preparation of this book.

Contents

Mysterious Magnetism

Magnets are strange. In everyday life they can serve as note-holders that stick pieces of paper to the refrigerator, paper-clip holders, or cupboard latches that keep doors closed.

Picky stickers

Magnets are mysterious because they work only on certain substances. A magnet is usually a small lump of metal that seems to grab certain items and stick to them with an invisible strength. Yet a magnet has no effect at all on other substances, such as wool, paper, wood, or glass.

Sticky spelling
Many of us played with magnets when we learned to read and spell. These magnetized letters can be stuck to metal surfaces. Although they stick firmly, they still can be moved easily.

An unseen force

Magnets are also mysterious because their force is invisible. The magnetic force, or magnetism, spreads out from a magnet, usually into the air, without showing itself. Sometimes we hold or move something near a magnet and it is grabbed as if by an unseen hand—this is magnetism at work. Magnetism works not only in air, but also under water, and even in the emptiness of a vacuum, where there is no air or anything else. Strong magnetism can also pass through thin layers of substances such as paper, cardboard, glass, or cloth. So, a magnet on one side of a sheet of cardboard can attract an object on the other side.

Magnetism is also difficult to understand. Usually it is explained in terms of the tiny particles, called atoms, that make up all objects and substances in the universe. The explanations of how magnetism works can get very technical. This is partly because scientists still do not fully understand the nature of magnets and their invisible forces. Also, the explanations are quite similar to the explanations of something else we use every day—electricity. Even in modern science, magnetism and electricity are sometimes confused.

Contents

Magnetism and history

Over 2,500 years ago, people in ancient Greece knew how a certain kind of rock, lodestone, would pull certain other kinds of rocks toward it. In some cases, if the other rock was another lump of lodestone, the two pieces would repel each other. Lodestone, today also called magnetite, is now known to be a mineral with natural magnetism. Since ancient times, magnetism has fascinated and puzzled people and been a challenge for scientists to explain.

Magnetism says "it's me"

An ATM card or credit card has a strip of magnetic particles that contains information about the owner. If the information does not match the security number entered by pressing the keys, the card does not work.

Magnetism and us

In modern life, magnetism is used far more widely, and in applications with much more practical value than refrigerator note-holders. It is needed for thousands of machines and gadgets from televisions, computers, and cell phones, to microwave ovens, cars, and medical scanners. Any equipment with an electric motor, from a bullet train to an electric toothbrush, uses magnetism.

Besides all these uses, magnets and magnetism are important away from daily life. For instance, magnetism is used in space and for exploring remote lands. It is even used for watching the northern and southern lights—the shimmering curtains of light in the night sky near the North and South poles. Magnets may be strange and mysterious, but they are very widespread and very useful. In fact, in our modern world we cannot get along without them.

Simple but Useful

Magnets are rarely obvious. This is especially true of permanent magnets in daily life. We rarely realize we are using them. They perform their tasks silently. Yet they are almost everywhere. In addition to the uses of permanent magnets described below, can you think of any others?

Everyday magnets
Many screwdrivers are also magnets, so they helpfully hold on to steel screws or lift them from holes.

Destroying magnetism

Most permanent magnets keep their magnetic force for many years, but not forever. The force fades with time and use. Knocking a magnet hard several times can cause its magnetism to disappear right away. If a permanent magnet is heated above a certain temperature, it loses its magnetism completely. The exact temperature at which this happens varies depending on which materials were used to make the magnet. It is called the Curie temperature, after French scientist Pierre Curie (1859–1906). For a typical everyday magnet made of iron-based steel, the Curie temperature is about 1380°F to 1470°F (750°C to 800°C).

Tools and utensils

Knives are sharp and dangerous and should be stored safely, especially in the kitchen. A magnetic knife holder has a long, striplike magnet that attracts the steel blades of knives. This keeps them safely out of the way. Magnetic door catches and closers on cupboards and refrigerators work in the same way.

When you open a tin can, the cut edge of the lid can also be dangerous. Many hand-powered and electrical can openers include a magnet that attracts the steel of the lid as it comes away from the rest of the can and holds it safely out of the way for careful disposal.

Steel-based pins, needles, nails, and screws have sharp points and can also cut us. If they are spilled on the floor, you can use a magnet to pick them up safely. If they fall into a crack or some other hard-to-reach place, a magnet on a string or bar can lift them out. Screwdrivers also have magnetic tips for holding the screws.

The ability of magnetism to pass through a thin layer of some substances and to work in water comes in handy when cleaning windows. A strong magnet is placed on one side of the glass. It attracts a metal layer inside the sponge or cloth on the other side of the glass. As the magnet is moved around, the sponge or cloth on the other side is pulled along the surface, wiping the glass clean. Magnetic cleaners like this are useful for places where people cannot reach, such as the outside of large windows in a high building.

Hold on tight
In travel chess, the pieces have small magnets in their bases. The magnets hold the pieces onto the metal board so they do not fall over in places like cars, trains, and buses.

Toys and games
Magnets are used in many toys and other products used for fun because of their stickiness. Plastic letters, numbers, and shapes can have small magnets on the back, so they can be stuck to a magnetic board or to an appliance such as a refrigerator. Some toy trains use magnets to join their cars. Fishing games use magnets on strings to catch the metal fish in a pretend pool. Sports games use magnets on sticks, which are put under the field to attract the magnetic bases of the players.

Features of a Magnet

Perhaps the most familiar type of magnet is the bar magnet. It is often shaped like a bar or rod, but a magnet can also be a square block, rounded disc, ring, ball, or horseshoe. This familiar kind of magnet is called a permanent magnet because its magnetic force is always present.

All shapes and sizes
Permanent magnets come in many designs and sizes, attracting each other and also steel objects, such as paper clips.

Attracted by a magnet

The standard bar magnet shows the basic features of any permanent magnet. It attracts or pulls certain objects, and they stick to it. An object that is attracted by a magnet is said to be magnetic. Many common substances, such as plastic, glass, paper, wood, wool, and pottery, are not magnetic. The most common magnetic substance is the metal iron. However, iron is rarely used in its pure form to make everyday objects. Usually it has carbon added to it. These two elements are used to make the metallic alloy called steel (or carbon steel), which is very common in daily life.

Hard and soft magnetic materials

Permanent magnets made of steel are usually hard. This does not refer to their physical hardness, but how long they keep their magnetism. Magnets are made by putting a piece of iron or steel into the very powerful force of another magnet. If the magnetism remains after the other magnetic force is taken away, then the substance is called hard. If the magnetism fades quickly, it is called soft. Hard magnets, which are the familiar permanent magnets, are usually made of steel. Soft magnets are usually made of iron. Soft magnets have many uses in electromagnets, electric motors, and electrical generators, as we will see in this book.

Farther = weaker

The strength of a magnet's force does not fade in a regular way with increasing distance from the magnet. It becomes much weaker, very quickly. If you double the distance from the magnet, you do not decrease the force by half, but by 8 times. If you triple the distance, the force decreases 27 times. Scientists call this the cube rule—2 cubed, or $2 \times 2 \times 2 = 8$, and 3 cubed, or $3 \times 3 \times 3 = 27$. This is why the pull of a magnet on a magnetic object does not seem very strong until the object is right next to it.

Two poles

Another feature of a magnet is that its magnetic force is strongest at two places called poles. A bar magnet has a pole at each end. We can feel this when the bar magnet attracts a magnetic item such as a paper clip. The clip is held most strongly at one pole. A horseshoe magnet is like a bar magnet bent around into a U shape, so its poles are closer together. This combines their magnetic force into a smaller area, so a suitably sized item can be held more strongly, with two poles instead of one. A disc-shaped magnet usually has a pole on each of the flat sides. The two poles are not the same. They are usually called north, or positive, and south, or negative.

Polar attraction
Magnetism is strongest at a magnet's poles. The poles are at the ends of this horseshoe magnet, so tiny pieces of iron filings stick mainly here.

What Is Magnetism?

It is fairly easy to describe what a magnet looks like and what it does. But why does a magnet have the special power of attracting certain objects, mainly those containing iron? The answer lies in the particles, called atoms, which make up all substances and all matter. Everything is made of atoms, but they are far too small to see. The spot of ink that forms the dot on this letter *i* contains more than 10 billion atoms.

Why iron?

The lining up of tiny magnetic domains cannot happen in just any substance. Each kind of pure substance or chemical element, such as iron, carbon, or aluminum, has its own type of atom. Each has a unique number of electrons and other subatomic particles. Iron has 26 electrons and this number, along with the pattern of the orbits and spins of the electrons, is best at producing a magnetic force. Iron-containing metals are also known as ferrous metals. So the ordinary type of magnetism, which attracts them, is called ferromagnetism.

Inside the atom

Atoms may be very, very small, but they are not the smallest things. Each atom is made of even tinier parts, called subatomic particles. There are three main kinds of subatomic particles—protons, neutrons, and electrons.

Protons and neutrons are at the center of an atom, grouped closely together into a bunch known as the nucleus. Electrons are much smaller and lighter, and they are outside the nucleus. They can be imagined as moving around the nucleus, almost like satellites orbiting planet Earth. The protons in all kinds of atoms are the same. So are the neutrons, and so are the electrons. What makes the difference between atoms of one substance, such as iron, and another, such as copper, is the number of these particles in each atom. Some atoms have just a few subatomic particles, while others have more than 200. Iron, the main magnetic substance, has 26 protons, 30 neutrons, and 26 electrons.

As the electrons move around the nucleus, they also spin around—like Earth, which turns like a top as it orbits the Sun. Electrons have a type of energy, or charge, called electric charge. As they spin and orbit, their moving electric charges make a magnetic force. The charge of an electron is termed negative. The charge of a proton is known as positive. In most atoms, the number of electrons is equal to the number of protons. So the two kinds of charges balance each other, and the atom as a whole is neither positive nor negative.

All lined up

However, moving charges make a magnetic force. So each atom, with its spinning, orbiting electrons, is like a tiny magnet with its own magnetic force. It has regions of greatest magnetic force, like two poles. In most substances, the magnetic forces of individual atoms do not line up. They face in different directions at random. So the billions of atoms in an object all have magnetic forces working in different directions, and they cancel each other out. There is no overall magnetic force. In a magnet, the magnetic forces of the atoms are all lined up, or aligned. They all face the same way. Their magnetism combines into larger areas called domains, which are like tiny bar magnets. The domains in turn combine to form the magnetic force of the whole magnet.

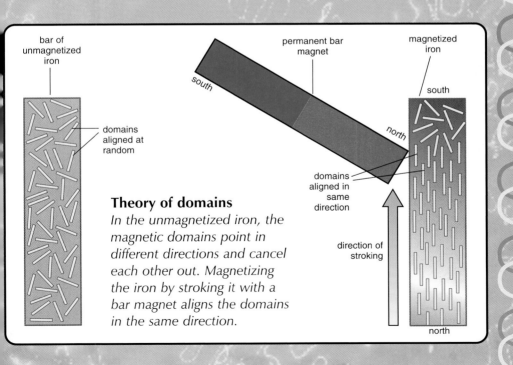

bar of unmagnetized iron

permanent bar magnet

magnetized iron

south

south

domains aligned at random

north

domains aligned in same direction

Theory of domains
In the unmagnetized iron, the magnetic domains point in different directions and cancel each other out. Magnetizing the iron by stroking it with a bar magnet aligns the domains in the same direction.

direction of stroking

north

The Magnetic Field

We can see the effects of magnetic force when a magnet attracts an object containing iron. We cannot, however, see the force itself. We can draw a diagram of the invisible magnetic force, which helps to explain where it is and what it does. The original idea for this came from English scientist Michael Faraday in the 1830s. Faraday did many experiments investigating magnetism and electricity. He also made early versions of many electrical-magnetic devices, such as the electric motor and electrical transformer.

The greatest experimenter

English scientist Michael Faraday (1791–1867) worked on electricity, magnetism, chemicals, forces, and many other areas of science. He was one of the greatest experts at building electrical devices and conducting experiments who ever lived. Beginning in the 1830s, he studied the connections between electricity and magnetism. Faraday became famous at the Royal Institution, a scientific society in London.

A field of magnetism

The region around a magnet where the magnetic force is present is called the magnetic field. The size of the magnetic field varies according to the size and the strength of the magnet. The magnetic field of a small but very powerful magnet may reach farther than that of a larger but weaker one. The magnetic field does not suddenly stop at a certain distance from the magnet. It fades away with distance, as we have seen. For example, the magnetic fields of everyday small bar magnets, such as those that hold notes to the refrigerator, extend outward about 2 to 3 inches (5 to 8 cm). Farther than a certain distance from the magnet, however, the field is so weak and ineffective that for practical purposes we can imagine it as zero.

Magnetic objects

When a piece of iron is placed in a magnetic field, the field makes the piece of iron into a magnet itself, by making its domains line up. This is known as magnetic induction. The piece of iron pulls on the real magnet, which pulls back. This is why an iron object is magnetic, or attracted to a magnet. As soon as the magnetic field is taken away, the domains of the piece of iron become jumbled again, and so it is no longer a magnet.

Magnetic field

Near the poles, the lines of magnetic force are closest, showing that the field is strongest there. Between the poles the lines spread out to show that the field is weaker.

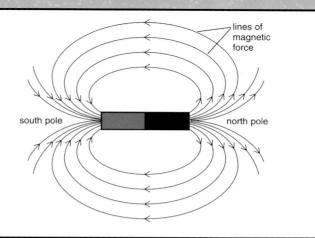

lines of magnetic force

south pole

north pole

Lines of force

A magnetic field is often drawn in a diagram by using lines that run from one pole of the magnet to the other. This is a useful idea, because the lines show that the magnetic field has a direction, from one pole to the other. It is also useful because a stronger magnetic field can be shown by making the lines closer together.

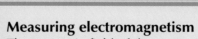

Measuring magnetism

The overall strength of a magnetic field, known as magnetic flux, is measured in units called webers. The number of webers shows the total force of the whole magnetic field around a magnet (see page 52). Another way to measure magnetism is in teslas. As we will see later, this shows the closeness of the lines of force in a particular part of the field.

Measuring electromagnetism

The magnetic field of the motor in an electric drill is measured, to see how it will stand up to bumps and wear and tear after it has been used a lot.

Not Just Iron

Iron is the main substance involved in magnetism. But other metals and materials are magnetic and can be made into magnets, too. One such substance is nickel, a very hard and shiny metal that is used to make coins. Another is cobalt, another hard metal, used in machine parts that have to be very tough. Less common materials that are magnetic are neodymium, gadolinium, and dysprosium. These materials belong to a group of substances called rare earth metals, or rare earths, because they were once thought to be rare in Earth's rocks. We now know that some of them are more plentiful that many other metals.

Mixed magnets

Many of the permanent magnets in daily use around the home and in machines are made of mixtures of various metals and other substances. These mixtures, or blends, are called alloys. The various kinds of steel are alloys of iron blended with carbon and usually additional metals. Scientists have spent many years testing various metals and alloys to see if they can make stronger magnetic materials. It is not only the strength of the magnet that is important, but also whether the magnetic material is tough and long lasting, can resist bumps or vibrations, and will keep its magnetism for a long time.

No hiding place
A new type of magnetic fingerprint powder for use in police investigations may give clearer prints more quickly than the traditional type. The inventor of this new method is British scientist Brian Wilshire.

Small, light sounds

Headphones have two large cuplike parts, one to fit over each ear. Inside each cup is a small version of a loudspeaker, with a powerful magnet. In the 1960s, scientists testing new magnetic materials invented samco, or samarium-cobalt. Permanent magnets made from it were small and light, yet very powerful. This allowed the development of earphones, in which the magnet and whole speakerlike device could be made small enough to fit into the ear.

Tiny magnets
Each earphone has a tiny magnet within a plastic case that can fit into the ear.

Types of magnetic material

In general, everyday types of permanent magnets are made from two groups of materials—non-rare earth and rare earth. The non-rare earth materials include alnicos and ceramics. Alnico (Al-Ni-Co) permanent magnets are a combination of the metals aluminum, nickel, and cobalt. They are not expensive to make, but they tend to lose their magnetism more easily than other types. Ceramic permanent magnets, also called hard ferrites, contain iron in the form of iron oxide. They also contain the substances strontium and barium. They can be powerful and cheap to make. But they are also very brittle, so they crack or splinter easily.

More power

The rare earth magnetic materials include samco or samarium-cobalt (Sm-Co), and neodymium-iron-boron (Nd-Fe-B). Magnets made from them tend to be expensive, but they have great power for their size. The ability of a substance to retain its magnetic field over a long period is called retentivity. The steel alloys used to make permanent magnets have high retentivity. They need a very strong magnetic field to make them magnetic, but when that field is taken away, they keep their magnetism very well for a long time.

Attract and Repel

If a magnet is put near a magnetic substance, the magnet attracts it. But what happens if a magnet is put near another magnet? One of two things. The two magnets may pull powerfully toward each other, or they may repel each other, also very strongly. This happens because the two poles of a magnet are not the same. They are opposite of each other. One pole is called the positive, +, or north pole. The other is known as the negative, –, or south pole. The names *north* and *south* were used by French scientist Peter Peregrinus in about 1280. At this time, magnets were becoming more common in the form of devices called magnetic compasses, used by sailors to find their way at sea.

Maglev

The pushing force between the like poles of two magnets, or the pulling force between unlike poles, can be strong enough to lift many people— and the train car they are riding in. These types of trains are called maglevs, which is short for *magnetic levitation*. It means using magnetic forces to lift, or levitate, an object so that it appears to float. In one system, magnets in the train repel magnets in the track, and the train levitates above the track. Maglevs are used in a few small-scale railway-type systems, mostly in city centers and at airports. They do away with noise, vibration, and wear or wheels. But they need a lot of electrical energy to make the magnetic fields because they use electromagnets (see page 28).

Japanese maglev train
Maglev trains give a smooth, quiet ride, but they need huge amounts of electricity to charge their electromagnets.

Like and unlike

Peregrinus found that if the north pole of one magnet is held near the north pole of another magnet, the two poles repel each other. If two south poles are put near each other, they also repel each other. If a south pole and a north pole are brought near each other, however, they attract. Peregrinus first came up with the rule we use today: "Like poles repel, unlike poles attract." This is important, not only in the study of magnetism but in using electricity and in many other areas of everyday science. A similar principle is used in electricity, where the same electric charges (such as two positives) repel, but positive and negative attract.

Magnetic induction

As described earlier, when a permanent magnet attracts a magnetic object, it causes, or induces, the object to become a magnet. This is only temporary, though. If the object is stuck to the magnet's north pole, the part of the object next to the north pole will temporarily become a south pole. The farthest part becomes a temporary north pole.

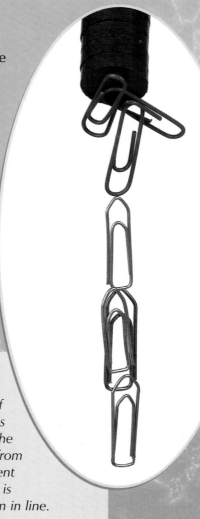

Then, if another magnetic object is brought near, the temporary, or induced, magnet will attract it, too, and so on. This is how a powerful magnet can pick up a whole chain of small objects such as paper clips or pins, as each one becomes a small temporary magnet. The magnetism becomes weaker at each link along the chain. If the clip closest to the permanent magnet is pulled off, the magnetism along the chain disappears and the chain falls apart.

Magnetic induction
This string of paper clips is passing on the magnetism from the permanent magnet that is holding them in line.

Magnetism and Electricity

Today we know that magnetism and electricity are related. In fact, they are parts of the same general force, electromagnetism. For hundreds of years, though, people either thought that they were the same thing— or that they were completely different.

Lodestone (magnetite)
This naturally magnetic rock was known in ancient times in Magnesia, now part of northern Greece.

The power to pull

In ancient Greece, it was known that substances such as amber could be given powers of attraction. Amber is the golden-colored resin, or sap, of ancient trees, preserved and hardened over millions of years. If a piece of amber was rubbed briskly with a cloth, it would attract lightweight objects such as feathers. Today this is explained as being a result of electrostatic charge, or static electricity. It is the same force that makes a blown-up balloon stick to the wall after it has been rubbed on clothing.

Different but the same

In the 1600s and 1700s, scientists carried out more experiments and began to find some of the differences between magnetism and electricity.

Why *magnet?*

The term *magnet* may come from the name of a region in Greece called Magnesia. This was part of Thessaly, which is now an area of northern Greece. The rock lodestone (magnetite), which has natural magnetism, was well known there. It lay on the ground looking like other rocks, and people were fascinated by its property of attraction.

In the 1820s, Hans Christian Oersted and André-Marie Ampère discovered very close links between magnetism and electricity, and how one could generate the other. In the 1870s, Scottish scientist James Clerk Maxwell explained mathematically how magnetism and electricity were both part of the same basic force, electromagnetism.

Magnetic and electric

A fire gives out light for us to see by. It also gives out heat to keep us warm. The fire is the same in both cases, but it can be described in two different ways, as bright or hot. Likewise, magnetism and electricity are two views of the same force, and one accompanies the other. Together they are called electromagnetism.

The electromagnetic force is found everywhere—within atoms, in our machines and gadgets, all around our planet Earth, even across the entire universe. It is one of the most basic forces known to science. However, the confusion between magnetism and electricity continued for a long time. In the year 1600, English scientist William Gilbert wrote a book about his experiments both with magnets, and with what we now call static electricity. He named his book *De Magnete,* or *About Magnets.* Perhaps this was not surprising, because the word *electricity* was almost unknown at the time. It had just been invented—by William Gilbert.

William Gilbert
William Gilbert was a brilliant researcher of magnetism.

Great Englishman

William Gilbert (1544–1603) worked in many areas of science. But his main job was doctor—England's royal physician for Queen Elizabeth I and King James I. Away from his patients, Gilbert was fascinated by magnetism. He studied how an iron object could be made into a magnet by stroking it with another magnet, and how heating a magnet made its magnetism disappear. He helped to prove that Earth was like a giant magnet. His book, *De Magnete* (1600), was read by famous scientists throughout Europe. It is often called the first great English scientific work

Magnetic Earth

What is the biggest magnet you have ever seen? Look around and outside, and you will see it—Earth. Our whole planet is a magnet. English scientist William Gilbert first realized this more than 400 years ago. Even so, Gilbert did not know how Earth makes its magnetism. Today the reason is clearer. The occurrence of the magnetic force is a result of the inner structure of the planet.

Deep inside Earth

Planet Earth is a giant ball about 7,900 miles (12,700 km) across. The outer layer of solid rock, the crust, is very thin. Below is a much thicker layer of partly melted rock, the mantle.

At the planet's center is a huge round core of iron and nickel. The core is under tremendous pressure and temperature—more than 5430°F (3000°C). As Earth spins, parts of the core flow slowly like thick molasses. The swirling motion of the iron makes electrical currents, which then produce magnetism, as explained on later pages.

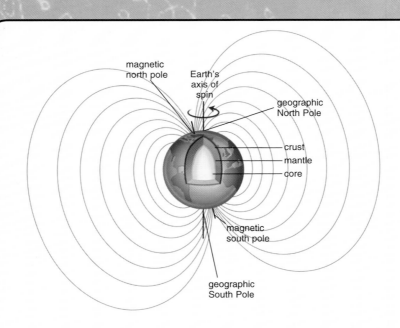

Earth's magnetic field
The magnetic lines of force curve from one magnetic pole to the other. These magnetic poles are some distance from the geographic North and South poles.

Earth's magnetic field

Earth's magnetic field has been mapped and measured in detail. The lines of magnetic force run from the top, or northern end, of Earth, around and down to the southern end. The place at each end where we can imagine all the lines of force coming together at their strongest, and heading down into the ground, is called the magnetic pole. The one in the northern region, or Arctic, is the magnetic north pole, and the one at the opposite end, in the Antarctic, is the magnetic south pole. These places and their importance are described further on the next page. Earth's magnetic field is not just on the surface. It is inside the planet and also extends far above it, up through the air and out into space.

Earth is not the only planet with magnetism. Other planets in space have it, and so do the Sun, other stars, and many other giant objects deep in space. Magnetism is present all across the universe.

How strong is Earth's magnetism?

The strength of a magnetic field within a certain area can be imagined as the closeness of its lines of force (as shown in the diagram opposite). The scientific name for this strength is magnetic flux density. It is measured in teslas. At a certain place on the planet's surface—say Washington, D.C.—Earth's magnetic field is 0.000057 teslas. The small permanent magnets in earphones are more than 1,000 times more powerful. (One tesla is equal to one weber per square meter.)

A varied field

Earth's magnetic field is not equally strong everywhere. It varies slightly, for a number of reasons. One is the amount of iron in the rocks. Rocks with a lot of iron tend to affect the Earth's lines of magnetic force. Very sensitive devices, called magnetometers, can measure these variations in magnetism. They help prospectors and surveyors find new sources of useful rocks and minerals.

Magnetism under water
Divers use magnetometers to map Earth's magnetism at various depths of water throughout the oceans.

Finding the Way

Earth's natural magnetic field can be used in many ways. One of the most common is finding directions, or navigating. The main device for doing this is the magnetic compass, or navigational compass. For hundreds of years people used magnetic compasses, without really understanding how they worked, to find their way across sea and land.

Age of discovery

Compasses were in use in ancient China about 2,200 years ago, and possibly well before this time. Those early compasses were made from the naturally magnetic rock called lodestone. From about the 1100s, compasses were used on ships to navigate across oceans, first by sailors from China, then in East Asia. By the 1300s, Europeans were using them, too. Magnetic compasses helped to open the way for the Age of Discovery, from the 1400s to the 1600s, when sailors explored distant lands and traveled all around the world.

A typical compass

A standard magnetic compass consists of a long, thin magnet, the needle. It is free to swing around, or pivot, usually on a sharp point near its middle. Each end, or pole, of the compass needle attracts the unlike pole of another magnet—Earth. The compass swings around so one end points to the Earth's magnetic north pole and the other end to the magnetic south pole.

Magnetic compass
A compass must be held level so the needle can turn easily to show north. Then the map will be held in the correct position to find the route.

Compass on board

On a ship, the compass floats in a bowl or bath of oil, so that it remains level and steady as the ship itself tilts in the waves. Back on dry land, compasses are also useful for everyday tasks, such as making sure a television antenna or dish points in the right direction to pick up the best signals.

Two norths and two souths?

The true, or geographic, North and South poles are the places around which Earth spins. Earth rotates on an imaginary line, its axis, every 24 hours. The geographic North and South poles are the ends of this axis. But a compass points to the magnetic north and south poles. These are where the lines of magnetic force are strongest. They are in different places from the geographic poles, because of the way Earth's magnetism is made deep in its core. Detailed maps are marked with directions for both the true and magnetic poles.

The magnetic north pole is near Bathurst Island, in northern Canada, about 810 miles (1,300 km) from the true North Pole.

The magnetic south pole is in the ocean off the coast of Wilkes Land, about 1,740 miles (2,800 km) from the true South Pole, in Antarctica.

Wanderings, Dips, and Flips

A magnetic compass needle does not always point directly at the north magnetic pole. Because of small-scale local changes in Earth's magnetic field, it may point a few degrees to the west (left, facing north) or east (right, facing north). These slight variations are partly a result of the iron content of the rocks in the area. High levels of iron in a rock tend to bend the lines of force into the rock, away from other rocks nearby that contain less iron. The difference in angle between the direction of the compass needle and the true direction of the north magnetic pole is called the angle of declination. It is marked on the very accurate maps used by sailors, pilots, explorers, surveyors, space scientists, and others, so they can take it into account.

Still important

Today, the magnetic compass has mostly been replaced by the Global Positioning System (GPS) for navigating. GPS is a series of satellites in space that beam radio signals down to receivers on Earth. Using a GPS receiver, a person can find true north and his or her position to the nearest 100 feet (30 m) or less. However, GPS receivers sometimes break down, run out of battery power, or fail to pick up the satellite signals. So people who travel in out-of-the-way places or navigate planes or boats still learn to use a magnetic compass.

The angle of dip

At the magnetic north and south poles, the lines of magnetic force go straight into the ground. As you travel away from either pole, the angle at which the lines enter the ground becomes lower. This angle at which the lines enter the ground is called inclination, or dip. It varies from 90 degrees at the magnetic poles to nearly 0 degrees at the equator. It is measured by an inclinometer, or dipometer, which is like a compass on its side. When pointed north–south, the inclinometer's magnetized needle swings to align itself with Earth's lines of magnetic force as they enter the ground. For example, in Washington, D.C., the angle of dip is 71 degrees. Small changes in both inclination and declination give clues to the kinds of rocks and minerals that might be underground.

Poles on the move

The magnetic north and south poles do not stay still. They move across the surface by up to several miles or kilometers each year. These wandering poles do not affect most travelers. They do mean, however, that the magnetic poles must be tracked and measured year by year, so that very accurate maps can be updated.

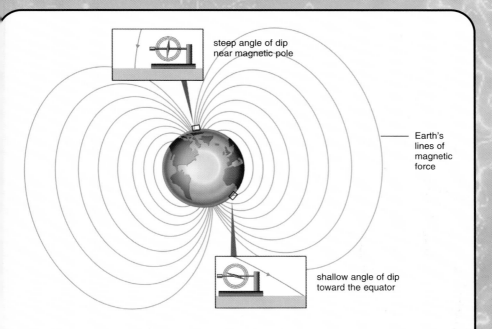

steep angle of dip
near magnetic pole

Earth's
lines of
magnetic
force

shallow angle of dip
toward the equator

Into the ground
The inclinometer, or dipometer, shows the angle at which Earth's lines of magnetic force enter the ground. This varies around the planet's surface, from the magnetic north pole to the magnetic south pole.

Flipping poles

In fact, at some point long ago, Earth's whole magnetic field flipped, or reversed. The magnetic north pole suddenly became the magnetic south pole, and vice versa. Exactly how this happened is not clear. But these magnetic reversals have happened many times over millions of years. We may be heading for another flip in the future, perhaps a thousand years from now. Scientific measurements also show that Earth's magnetic field is now less than half as strong as it was 10,000 years ago.

Magnetic Skies

The air around us and the skies above are filled with various forms of magnetism, but most of them are invisible. They include Earth's own magnetic field, which extends huge distances from the surface, up through the air of the atmosphere and out into space.

Animals and magnetism

Many animals travel on long-distance journeys called migrations. Some probably use magnetism to help them find their way. They also use other navigating methods, such as the positions of the Sun, Moon, and stars, and landmarks, such as mountains and rivers. These animals include many birds, including swifts, swallows, geese, and swans, and whales, sea turtles, and such fish as salmon and eels. These creatures may be able to sense Earth's magnetic field using tiny particles of iron-containing minerals in their bodies.

Built-in compass?
Animals such as these migrating humpback whales may have a natural sense of magnetism.

Magnetism in space

More magnetism is made in the upper atmosphere in addition to the magnetic field from within Earth. This magnetism is a result of the solar wind—a continuous stream of various rays and fast-moving particles coming from the Sun. The solar wind hits Earth's own magnetic field and the outer parts of the atmosphere at heights of more than 60 miles (100 km) above the surface, and makes extra magnetic forces. These have only about 1/500th of the strength of the magnetic field from inside Earth. The whole area of magnetism around the planet is called the magnetosphere. It is shaped not like a ball, but like a pear, or teardrop. The blunt end faces the Sun and is about 31,000 miles (50,000 km) above Earth. The tapering end faces away from the Sun and is hundreds of times longer.

Storms and crackles

The magnetosphere is huge, far away and complicated, but it affects our daily lives in various ways. Magnetic storms occur when the solar wind changes, perhaps gaining strength for a time, and disturbs Earth's magnetic field. Magnetic storms do not usually affect the ordinary weather of winds, clouds, and rain. But they do affect radio waves and similar waves, which themselves are partly magnetic in nature. Such storms interfere with television and radio programs, causing crackles and fuzzy pictures. They also affect radio and microwave signals going up and down to satellites. This can disrupt long-distance telephone calls and navigation by planes and ships. Magnetic storms may also cause surges of electricity in the long power lines that cross the countryside, perhaps leading to power outages.

Magnetic lights

The auroras, or northern and southern lights, are huge, shimmering, multicolored curtains of light that sometimes appear high in the night sky. They occur most often in the far north and south, near the poles, at heights of between 30 and 190 miles (50 and 300 km). They are made when Earth's magnetic field grabs rays and particles of the solar wind and pulls them toward its most powerful areas of magnetism, near the poles. The rays and particles collide with Earth's own particles in the atmosphere and give out twinkles of light. The aurora borealis is seen in the far north, and the aurora australis in the far south.

Shining lights
The southern lights, or aurora australis, are the result of tiny particles from the Sun colliding with Earth's magnetic forces.

Electrical Magnets

The magnetism of a permanent magnet, such as an ordinary bar magnet, is present all the time. The magnetic field of an electromagnet, on the other hand, can be turned on and off. The magnetic field of both of these types of magnets works in exactly the same, it is most concentrated at the poles. And, as in a permanent magnet, like poles repel and unlike poles attract.

Sorting for recycling

An electromagnet, like a permanent magnet, attracts mainly iron-containing substances, such as steel. In a scrapyard or recycling center, it is important to sort out the steel and other iron-based metals, called ferrous metals, from other metals, such as aluminum, brass, and tin. An electromagnet can do this. As various metal objects pass by, the ferrous ones stick to the electromagnet. They are sent for recycling at the iron factory or steelworks. The aluminum and other metals continue on into different containers, since they need different methods of recycling.

Metal grab
Big magnets like this are used to lift, move, and drop ferrous metals.

On and off

An electromagnet uses electricity to make magnetism. Whenever a flow of electricity, known as electric current, passes along a wire, this makes a magnetic field around the wire. It happens because electricity is the movement along the wire of the tiny parts of atoms called electrons. In a permanent magnet, the magnetic force comes from the spinning and orbits of electrons within their atoms.

In an electromagnet, the magnetic force also comes from moving electrons. But these electrons are jumping from one atom to the next, along the wire. The instant that the electricity flows, the magnetic field forms around the wire. And the instant electricity stops, the magnetic field disappears.

Wound into a coil

The magnetic field around a single straight wire is very weak. It can be made much stronger by curling the wire into a coil called a solenoid. Coiling the wire brings together the magnetic fields around each turn of the coil, so they reinforce each other. The more coils, the stronger the magnetic field. Also the more powerful the electricity, measured as a higher voltage, the stronger the magnetic field.

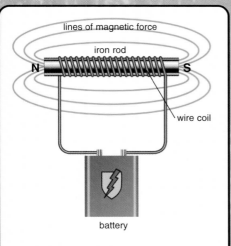

lines of magnetic force

iron rod

N S

wire coil

battery

Poles at the end
The core of an electromagnet has lines of force, like those of a bar-shaped permanent magnet, with the most powerful magnetism at the ends.

The core in the middle

Another way to concentrate the magnetism is to put a rod of iron along the middle of the coil. This is called the core of the solenoid. The lines of magnetic force from the coil flow through the core and, by magnetic induction, make it work like a bar magnet. The core will attract magnetic items, repel the like pole of another magnet and attract its unlike pole—but only while the electricity flows. Making the electricity flow the other way through the coil reverses the magnetic poles of the core.

Electromagnets are used in hundreds of everyday machines and gadgets, as shown on the following pages.

Making Electricity with Magnets

When electricity flows through a wire as moving electrons, as explained on the previous page, a magnetic field is created around the wire. This is called the electromagnetic effect. The opposite is also true. When a magnetic field moves near a wire, electricity is made to flow through the wire. The moving magnetism affects the electrons in the wire and makes them jump or flow along, which creates the current. This principle is called electromagnetic induction. It is an important part of the workings of thousands of machines, devices, and gadgets.

Twang!

Most kinds of electric guitars rely on electromagnetic induction. The metal guitar strings pass over a magnetic pickup, which contains a powerful bar magnet with a wire coil wound around it. When the string is plucked, it vibrates in the magnetic field of the bar magnet. This alters or distorts the field and moves its lines of force—which move in relation to the coil and so induce an electric current. A typical guitar magnetic pickup has a coil with more than 10,000 turns—the wire is very, very thin!

Magnetic music
The pickups under the strings on this electric guitar use magnetism to produce an electric current.

The need for change

In the electromagnetic effect, an electric current simply has to flow through a wire. There is no need for any movement of the wire or iron core. In electromagnetic induction, there is. If the magnet and wire stay still, then no electricity flows. There is a need for the magnet and the nearby wire to move in relation to each other. The wire can stay still as the magnet moves, or vice versa, or both can move. Like other features of magnetism and electricity, this can be explained in terms of electrons, which have their own tiny amounts of magnetism. As the magnetic field moves, it pushes the electrons along the wire, producing the electric current. If the magnet and the wire stay still in relation to each other, nothing happens.

Another change

Another choice besides the magnet and wire moving in relation to each other is the magnetic field changing strength. This is done using an electromagnet and feeding more or fewer volts through its coil. If the field becomes stronger or weaker, this induces a current to flow in a nearby wire, even if both the electromagnet and wire stay still.

Many uses

Electromagnetic induction is mentioned on many pages in this book, as part of the workings of microphones and motors. One of its main uses for daily life is in generators—machines that make electricity. In basic design, a generator has coils that are made to spin around in a magnetic field. This induces or generates electricity in the wires of the coils. The electricity supplied to our homes is produced in this way, by huge generators at power plants.

Magnetic wires in the road

Another common use of magnetism and electromagnetic induction is to control traffic lights. A series of wires is buried in the road, a few yards or meters in front of the lights. The thin channels made for the wires can often be seen as zigzag marks across the road surface. A small electric current flows through the wire, making a magnetic field around it. As a vehicle passes over, its metal parts affect the field and alter the current, which is detected by the light control system. So the traffic lights changes if there are vehicles waiting.

Useful Electromagnets

Electromagnets are made in all shapes and sizes, from smaller than the dot on this letter *i* to bigger than a house. Some are powered by electricity from batteries. Others use the higher voltage from the main electricity supply. An advantage of the electromagnet is that it can be made much more powerful than a permanent magnet of the same size. This is done by having thousands of turns of wire in the coil, and by passing more volts of electricity through the wire. Some of the most common big electromagnets are used in ironworks, steelyards, and scrapyards. They can pick up girders of steel weighing many tons or lift the steel-containing engine or body of a scrap car.

Sliding core

In some electromagnets, the core, which is an iron bar, is inserted into the coil. In another design, the core is free to slide in and out of the coil. When the electricity is turned on, if the core is not in the middle of the coil, but poking out of one end, the coil's magnetic field pulls it powerfully into the middle. In this way, electricity is turned into magnetism, which is then turned into a sliding motion. This sliding-core solenoid is therefore said to turn electrical energy into mechanical energy, or the energy of motion. The solenoid produces sliding-along or back-and-forth (reciprocating) motion. An electric motor does the same. But it produces spinning, or rotary, movement.

Start the car

The sliding-core solenoid design is used in many everyday devices, from doorbells to vehicles. One of the most common uses is for starting a vehicle. When the key is turned, electricity is sent through a solenoid near the engine called the starter solenoid. Attached to the core of this solenoid is a heavy-duty electrical contact designed to handle a large current. When the core slides along, it turns on the heavy-duty electrical contact with a small click. This sends a huge current to the powerful electric motor, called the starter motor. This gets the engine turning so that it can start to run under its own power.

Unlock the car

The central locking system of a car uses four or five solenoids. To lock the doors, the car key switches on electricity to a solenoid inside each door. This pulls its core into it, and the core is attached to the locking mechanism, which slides along to work the door lock. To unlock, the electricity flows to another solenoid, next to the first one. This pulls the core back to slide the locking mechanism the other way.

Sliding magnets
In a car with automatic locks, turning the key switches on electricity to several solenoids, one in each door, which then work the locks.

Ding-dong

In a doorbell with chimes that go "ding-dong," pressing the doorbell button makes electricity flow through a solenoid, which pulls the sliding iron core into it. As this happens, one end of the solenoid hits one chime to make the "ding." When the doorbell button is released, the electricity stops and the core is released. A spring pulls the core back out of the solenoid, and the core's other end hits the other chime to make the "dong."

A similar system is used for a remote-controlled door lock, as described in the panel on this page. This kind of flip-flop, or in-out, solenoid system is also used in many toys and games, such as radio-controlled cars and planes.

Sounds Magnetic

Every time we listen to a radio or television or to a music system, we hear sounds that are made with the help of magnets. This is because magnets are important parts of loudspeakers. Most loudspeakers use both permanent magnets and electromagnets.

Inside a speaker

Inside the cabinet or casing, the basic design of the speaker itself is a funnel shape called the cone or, sometimes, the diaphragm. This is the part we can see from the front, as a round, dark cone behind the cloth cover or metal grill. The cone has a coil of wire attached at the narrow end behind it. This wire

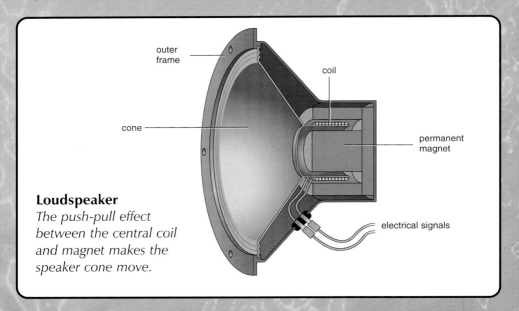

outer frame

coil

cone

permanent magnet

electrical signals

Loudspeaker
The push-pull effect between the central coil and magnet makes the speaker cone move.

coil, sometimes called the voice coil, is wound onto a ring-shaped piece of thin cardboard or plastic. The voice coil usually fits inside or into a round slot within a powerful permanent magnet. This permanent magnet is shaped like a ring or U and is usually very heavy. In a typical speaker, almost half the total weight is the permanent magnet.

Back and forth very fast

Wires bring electricity from the sound system to flow through the wire coil. As the electricity flows, it turns the coil into an electromagnet with its own magnetic field. This field attracts or repels the field of the permanent magnet, depending on which way the electricity flows.

The attracting and repelling forces pull and push the coil and make it move back and forth. The coil is attached to the cone, so the cone moves back and forth, or vibrates, as well. This happens hundreds or thousands of times each second. The vibrations of the cone produce sound waves, which travel out into the air.

Speaker in reverse

A loudspeaker changes electrical signals into sounds. A microphone does the reverse, and it works in the opposite way. In a moving-coil microphone, sound waves hit a thin, flexible sheet, or diaphragm, under the protective mesh. This sheet is the equivalent of the cone in the loudspeaker. A small coil of wire is attached to it, with a strong permanent magnet nearby. As sound waves vibrate the diaphragm and coil, the coil moves in the field of the permanent magnet. This causes varying amounts of electricity to flow in the wire of the coil. The pulses of electricity produced are electrical copies of the sounds coming into the microphone.

Moving to the music

Vinyl discs are used by many club DJs (disc jockeys) for music events. The disc has sounds stored as patterns of tiny waves in a long groove in the record's surface. A stylus, or needle, runs along this groove, and the waves make it vibrate. The stylus sticks out from a boxlike part smaller than a thumb, called the pickup. The pickup works in a similar way to a microphone. Inside the pickup, the other end of the stylus has tiny coils of wire attached to it, and these coils are next to a permanent magnet. Vibrations of the stylus make the wire coils move in the magnetic field. This produces electrical signals in the wire coils, which are fed to the sound system.

Pickup sounds
This DJ is scratching— moving a record back and forth—to achieve the sound he is looking for.

Looks Magnetic

Without magnets and electromagnetism, we would have no TV or computer screens. At least, we would not have the traditional types of screens, which are glass-fronted and heavy. They are often called tubes, or cathode ray tubes (CRTs).

Testing a television
This engineer is watching two screens. The large one on the upper right is the television being tested. The smaller one on the middle left is an oscilloscope, showing waves of electric current. Both screens use various combinations of electricity and magnetism.

Guns and screens

The basis of the CRT is a large glass container. It is nicknamed the tube, but it is more usually shaped like a funnel. At the narrow end are parts called electron guns. Electron guns have small metal wires or plates. They become very hot and send out electrons—the tiny parts of atoms that produce both magnetic fields and electric currents. The guns fire billions of electrons every second along the inside of the tube. The electrons hit the inner surface of the far end, which is the screen.

On the screen, the electrons hit tiny dots of chemicals called phosphors, which coat the inside of the screen. When the dots are hit, they glow with light. We see this light from the other side of the clear glass screen as the television or computer image. In color television, there are three colors of dots—red, green, and blue.

Scanning

What is the role of magnets in all this? Moving electrons make magnetism, and moving electrons can be affected by a magnetic field. In one design of television or computer screens, around the middle of the glass tube are sets of electromagnets. These are sometimes called focusing coils or deflector coils. Their magnetic fields affect the electrons whizzing past inside the tube. The magnetic fields make the electrons change direction, or deflect, according to how the electromagnets switch on and how much electricity passes through them. In this way the beam of electrons from a gun can be made to angle up and down and side to side.

The beam of electrons starts by hitting an upper corner of the screen. The electromagnets make the beam move in a line across the top of the screen. Then they do the same thing a tiny bit lower down the screen, and so on. This happens line by line, from side to side, all the way down the screen. This is called scanning.

Too fast to see

Scanning happens so fast that the whole screen is covered with hundreds of lines in less than one twentieth of a second. Our eyes cannot see the patterns of dots building up line by line. The pattern forms an image on the screen. This fades almost as soon as it forms. Then the same thing happens for the next picture on the screen, and so on, more than twenty pictures each second. Again, it all occurs so fast that our eyes blend the pictures, and they seem to be moving.

Magnetic screen

On some television and computer screens, stray areas of magnetism and static electricity gradually build up on the glass tube and other parts. These areas can make the picture blurred and oddly colored. They may also cause flickering and crackling. Some screens have a button to create a surge of magnetism that cleans the stray areas. Or this can happen automatically when the set is switched on or off. This is called degaussing.

Moving by Magnetism

One of our most useful everyday machines uses magnetism—the electric motor. Early types of motors were invented in the 1830s by British scientist Michael Faraday and American physicist Joseph Henry. A typical house today may have more than a hundred of them. One type is used in small battery-powered devices, from electric toothbrushes to laptop computers. It is called the DC, or direct current motor, because the battery that powers it makes an electric current that flows constantly in one direction.

Pioneer of electrical magnetism

American scientist and inventor Joseph Henry (1797–1878) trained first to become a watchmaker, and then a playwright and actor. Then after he read a popular science book, he decided to take up the subject. In 1832 he became a lecturer at the College of New Jersey (later Princeton University). Henry made great improvements to the design of electromagnets and early electric motors. In 1846 he became the first director of the Smithsonian Institution.

DC motor

The DC motor has both electromagnets and permanent magnets. In the simplest design, the electromagnet is a coil of wire on a long rod, called the shaft, which can spin around. The coil is sometimes called the armature of the motor. It is placed between the two ends of a U-shaped permanent magnet.

Electricity passes through the coil of wire and turns it into an electromagnet. The direction of the electricity means that the north pole of the electromagnet is next to the north pole of the permanent magnet, and the south pole of the electromagnet is next to the permanent magnet's south pole. Like poles repel, and as they push away from each other they cause the coil to spin around half a turn on its shaft. This brings the north pole of the permanent magnet and the south pole of the electromagnet nearer as they attract each other.

Switching poles

Electricity is fed to the coil through two parts called brushes. The brushes press from either side onto a ring-shaped part on the shaft, called the

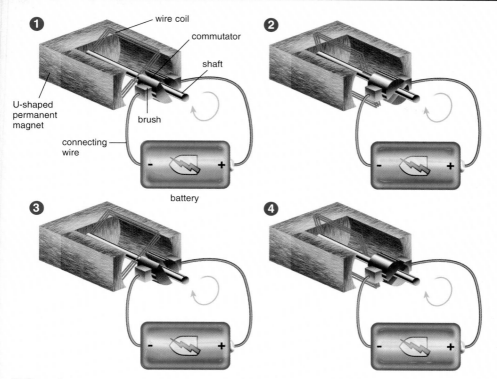

❶ wire coil / commutator / shaft / U-shaped permanent magnet / brush / connecting wire / battery

❷

❸

❹

DC motor

For each turn of a DC motor, the electric current is reversed by a rotating switch called the commutator. This makes the coil into an electromagnet with poles that reverse as it turns. The push-pull interaction with the permanent magnet keeps the coil spinning.

commutator. The commutator is actually in two halves, each connected to an end of the wire that forms the coil. As the coil spins half a turn, the commutator does, too. As the half-rings move around, each is pressed by the brush on the opposite side. This makes the electricity flow the other way through the coil, which reverses the coil's north and south poles. The permanent magnet stays the same. So again, like poles are near each other, and they repel. The shaft spins—but after another half turn, the commutator reverses the electricity again, and so on. In this way, the spinning continues and the motor goes around.

Many pushes and pulls

In most real motors, there are several coils of wire on the shaft and the commutator is split into many segments. This means the magnetic attractions and repulsions happen many times for each turn of the motor. This gives a smoother and more powerful turning force.

More About Motors

In a typical house there are motors in all kinds of appliances, from washing machines and freezers to electric screwdrivers and can openers. They run on electricity from the main supply. This is not direct current, or DC, as is electricity from a battery. It is alternating current, or AC. AC current changes, or alternates, its direction of flow, going one way and then the other, many times each second. Alternating current is used for main electricity partly because it can drive a type of powerful electric motor called an induction motor. Direct current cannot do this. The AC induction motor is usually quieter and more reliable because it does not have brushes and a commutator. These are the parts that wear out quickest in a DC motor. Other types of AC motors use brushes and bushes, or slip-rings.

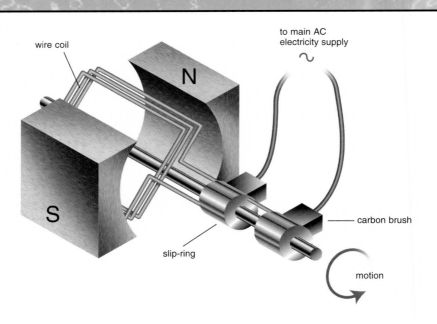

wire coil

to main AC
electricity supply

N

S

carbon brush

slip-ring

motion

Brush-type AC motor
The noninduction AC motor has padlike brushes, similar to a DC motor. These press-on, collar-shaped slip-rings (bushes) pass electricity to the coil. As the current flows one way then the other, the motor spins once.

Two sets of coils

The AC induction motor has a set of wire coils. These coils work as electromagnets that are mounted on a shaft and can spin around. This part of the design is similar to that of the DC motor. But the AC induction motor has no permanent magnets around the outside. Instead it has more wire coils that are arranged in a ring. The inner set of coils, which can spin, is called the rotor. The outer set, which stays still, is known as the stator. To make the motor work, alternating current is fed through the coils of the stator, but not all at the same time. The electricity is timed so that it produces a magnetic field in each coil in turn, in very fast succession. The effect is that the magnetic field hops from one coil to the next, so that it seems to go around and around the stator.

Magnetic speed

The first vehicles to hold the world land speed record, in the 1890s, were cars powered by electric motors. These electric cars reached speeds of up to 65 miles (105 km) per hour. But starting in about 1900, gasoline engines, and then jet engines, were used to power record-breaking cars. Today's land speed record for a car powered by an electric motor is 244 miles (393 km) per hour. This is only one-third the speed of the fastest jet-powered cars.

Rotor and stator

The coils of the rotor do not receive electricity along wires. But as the magnetic field goes around and around the stator, this makes electricity flow in the coils of the rotor, by induction. This electricity turns the coils of the rotor into electromagnets, and they attract or repel the magnetic field of the stator. The movement of the stator's magnetic field is carefully timed so that it drags the rotor with it, and so the rotor spins around.

DC and AC motors are called electric motors. But magnetism is equally important. A better name might be magnetic-electric motors, or perhaps electric-magnetic motors. Although modern motors are reliable, they do sometimes break down or wear out. The problem often begins with the machinery attached to the motor. The machinery becomes worn or stiff, so the motor has to produce more turning force to make the machinery work. As the strain on the motor increases, it has to turn more slowly and with greater force. More magnetism is needed to do this, which means that more electric current flows through the wire coils. More current and slower rotation makes heat build up in the coils. Eventually the motor burns out.

Micro-Magnetism

Magnetism can be used to push, pull, slide, spin, lift, turn—and store. Writing is a way of storing information as marks on paper. In the same way, information can be recorded as patches of magnetism in a magnetic substance, known as the magnetic medium. The patches of magnetism cannot be seen because they are far too small. And in any case, magnetism is not visible. Besides this, the magnetic patches do not make shapes like letters and words on paper. The patterns of magnetism are more like lines or dots with spaces between. They are a code for the information. However, the principle is similar to that of writing. Keeping information this way is known as magnetic data storage. It is likely that you use it every day, as we will see later in this book.

Write

How is information recorded on a magnetic medium and then read again for use? The key part is the read-write head. One basic design for this is a tiny U-shaped piece of metal called a yoke, with wire coils around it. If electricity flows through the coils for a tiny fraction of a second, they turn the yoke into an electromagnet.

The magnetic field across the gap of the yoke is close to the surface of the magnetic medium. The field affects the tiny magnetic particles of the medium and makes them flip to form a patch of magnetism. It is like giving many tiny bar magnets a certain direction, or alignment.

Small head
The tiny read-write head of a computer magnetic hard disc is at the narrow end of the swinging arm, on the lower left of the picture. It rests on the disc's surface layer of magnetic particles.

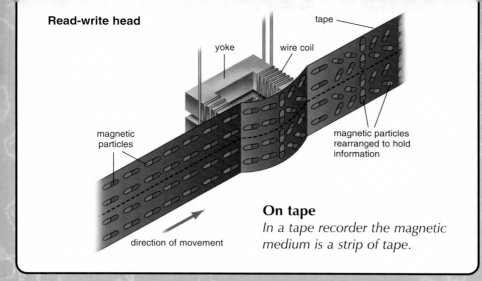

Read-write head

yoke

wire coil

tape

magnetic particles

magnetic particles rearranged to hold information

direction of movement

On tape
In a tape recorder the magnetic medium is a strip of tape.

During this time, the magnetic medium is moving past the read-write head. So the head writes a tiny patch of magnetism on it, then another one slightly farther along, and so on. Information consists of millions of these tiny patches written as the medium moves past the head.

Read

To obtain stored information, the medium again moves past the read-write head. As a patch of magnetism goes past, it produces a tiny electrical current in the wire coils, by electromagnetic induction. So as the medium moves, the head picks up the patterns and spaces of the patches and feeds the electrical signals to other parts of the machine.

The smaller the patches of magnetism, the more information can be stored in an area. Similarly, the faster the medium moves past the head, the more patches can be stored per second, so the total amount of information is greater. In some designs, the read and write heads are two separate devices.

So much information

Engineers are gradually packing more and more information onto magnetic storage media. Today, tens of billions of patches can be stored in an area smaller than a fingernail. If you tried to write these patches as zeroes on paper, you would need a piece of paper 0.8 square miles (2 km²). Engineers hope one day to be able to store all the information for the pictures and sounds of a full-length movie on a patch of magnetic medium the size of this *0*.

Magnetic Media

Recording
Digital video cameras use magnetic tapes to store information.

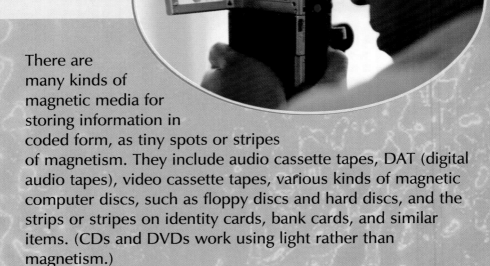

There are many kinds of magnetic media for storing information in coded form, as tiny spots or stripes of magnetism. They include audio cassette tapes, DAT (digital audio tapes), video cassette tapes, various kinds of magnetic computer discs, such as floppy discs and hard discs, and the strips or stripes on identity cards, bank cards, and similar items. (CDs and DVDs work using light rather than magnetism.)

Most of these magnetic media have the same basic structure. There is a base layer. For a tape, the base layer is a type of flexible plastic. But for a disc it is stiffer. On this is a magnetic layer, which contains billions of tiny grains of magnetic material. On the top is the shiny surface layer, which both protects the magnetic layer underneath and allows the read-write head to skim across without wear or scratching.

Tapes and discs

One problem with magnetic tape of any kind is that it must be wound along past the read-write head. So finding a particular piece of information at the end of the tape, if the tape is positioned near the beginning, takes time as the tape winds along. Another problem is known as print-though. When a tape is wound onto its spool or reel, the spiral windings of the tape press against each other. The tiny patches of magnetism in one winding of the tape are very close to the patches of the windings on either side of it. If the tape is not used for a long period, and stays tightly wound, the patches on adjacent windings can disturb and change each other.

Danger of destruction

In all forms of magnetic storage, a powerful magnetic field nearby can destroy the stored information by disrupting the magnetic patches. Sources of powerful magnetic fields include the permanent magnets of loudspeakers and the electromagnetic coils of motors and television sets. Leaving a magnetic tape or disc next to these can destroy the information. So can excessive heat or physical bumps and vibrations—just as in an ordinary bar magnet.

A magnetic disc gets around the lengthy problem of winding. The read-write head is on an arm and can swing from the outside of the disc across to its center, like the magnetic pickup for a vinyl record turntable. At the same time, the disc spins 100 or more times each second. With the swinging arm and spinning disc, the information on a particular part of the disc can be reached in a few thousandths of a second. In a computer hard drive, there is usually not one disc, but a stack of ten or more, each 2 to 4 inches (5 to 10 cm) across, with a space above each one for a swinging arm with its own read-write head. The head is positioned just 20 millionths of one millimeter from the surface of its disc. At such tiny distances, a speck of dust would seem like a huge boulder. So computer hard drives are sealed inside airtight boxes to keep dust out.

Swipe-read

The magnetic strips on security and bank cards also use tiny patches of magnetism. These are read by a swipe machine. The card's magnetic strip moves past a read head, which detects the magnetism by electromagnetic induction.

Magnetic key
Some locked doors are opened by cards rather than keys. The cards' magnetic code works a solenoid to undo the lock.

Electromagnetic Waves

We have seen how electromagnetism is a vital part of everyday devices. It is also all around us as different kinds of waves and rays.

Carrying information

Electromagnetic waves include radio waves, which carry information to our radios, broadcast television channels, and cell phones. Radio waves are also sent up to satellites in space, which beam them back down to different areas on Earth. They are also used in radar systems, which beam out pulses of radio waves and then pick up and analyze the echoes that bounce off objects. Radar is used by planes, ships, and weather satellites and in many other important ways.

Waves from space
Optical telescopes see light from space. Radio telescopes (above) detect radio waves from space. They are dish-shaped, like the dishes that receive satellite radio signals.

Two waves in one

It is difficult to picture an electromagnetic wave. It can be thought of as not one typical up-and-down, wavy line-type wave, but two. One of these contains magnetic energy. The other wave is at right angles to the first and contains the electrical energy. Each kind of wave has an equal amount of energy. This is indicated by the height of its peak or the depth of its trough. Both the magnetic and the electrical waves build to an upper peak at the same time. Then they fade away to zero, fall to their troughs, and rise again to zero—all the time staying in step with each other.

Electromagnetic waves travel incredibly fast, at the speed of light, which is about 186,300 miles (300,000 km) per second. Light is one type of electromagnetic wave.

The electromagnetic spectrum

There are many other kinds of electromagnetic waves, in addition to radio waves. They form a whole range, or spectrum, also known as electromagnetic radiation. They include:

- Microwaves, which are used not only for cooking but also for carrying information, in the same way as radio waves. They are sent between tall towers and beamed up and down to satellites in space.
- Infrared waves, or rays, which carry heat energy. The warmth of the Sun is a result of its infrared waves traveling to us through space.
- Light rays, which we sense with our eyes.
- Ultraviolet waves. Like light and infrared, these also come from the Sun. UV can burn and damage the skin.
- X rays, used in medicine to see inside the body, and also for many scientific purposes.
- Gamma rays, which are used on certain kinds of foods and other objects to sterilize them (kill all the germs on them).

How long are the waves?

In the electromagnetic spectrum, radio waves are the longest. Their wavelengths vary from several miles or kilometers to less than a yard or meter. Microwaves are mostly from 0.4 to 40 inches (10 to 1,000mm) long. Next shortest are infrared waves, with hundreds in 0.04 inch (1 mm). Then come light waves, with wavelengths of less than 0.000004 inch (0.001 mm). Even shorter are ultraviolet waves, and then X rays. Shortest of all are gamma rays. A million million gamma waves joined together would only stretch 0.04 inch (1 mm).

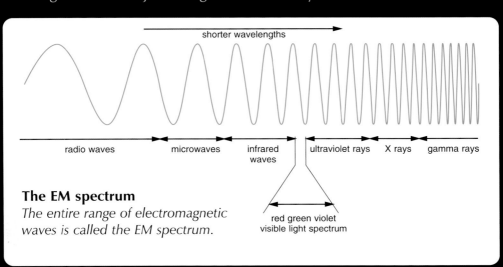

shorter wavelengths

radio waves | microwaves | infrared waves | ultraviolet rays | X rays | gamma rays

red green violet
visible light spectrum

The EM spectrum
The entire range of electromagnetic waves is called the EM spectrum.

Magnetic Medicine

Magnetism is used in health and medicine in several ways. X rays are incredibly short electromagnetic waves. They can pass through softer parts of the body, such as muscles and blood vessels. But they cannot pass through harder, denser parts, especially bones. So X-ray images are used to check for broken bones and for other health problems, such as certain kinds of growths or tumors. However, too much exposure to X rays can damage the body, so these ordinary, or plain, X rays are used carefully and in a very limited way.

CT scans

Another way to see inside the body using X rays is with a CT, or computerized tomography, scanner (also called CAT, or computerized axial tomography). This uses very weak and harmless X rays, which are beamed through the body at different angles and positions and sensed by detectors on the other side. A computer analyzes the results and builds up a picture of the body's internal parts, including soft ones such as blood vessels and nerves.

MR scans

MRI, or magnetic resonance imaging, is another form of diagnostic imaging. In MRI, a picture is made of what is happening inside the body, to identify or diagnose a problem. A person is placed in a large tunnellike scanner that contains huge sets of ring-shaped electromagnets.

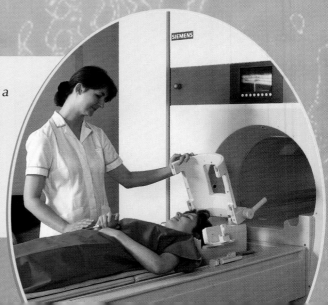

MR scanner
This person is about to enter a magnetic resonance scanner. The ring-shaped magnets are inside the machine's casing, and their holes form a tunnel in which the person lies on a sliding bed.

These electromagnets produce a very powerful magnetic field, almost 100,000 times stronger than Earth's natural magnetism. The field is so strong that all objects that could be magnetic must be kept well away, or they could be attracted from some distance and fly through the air to stick to the machine. Such objects include jewelry worn by the patient or the scanner operators. If an MRI magnet attracted a metal belt buckle, it would be very difficult to pull the buckle away again.

Magnetic diagnosis
A doctor examines MRI scans of the brain on a backlit screen, to identify or diagnose illness.

The intense magnetism of the scanner affects many of the atoms in the body and causes them to line up, like billions of tiny magnetic compass needles. Then a pulse of radio waves is fired into the body as the magnetic field is changed. The lined-up atoms respond by wobbling out of line, which makes them give off their own tiny radio pulses. Detectors in the machine receive these. Then they are analyzed by a computer to build up a detailed picture of internal body parts.

Is magnetism harmful?

We live constantly in Earth's magnetic field. However some scientists worry that stronger magnetism may cause harm. Several scientific studies have tried to find out if electromagnetic waves—for example, the radio waves to and from a cell phone—might affect the brain. There is no clear evidence yet. But in case there is a link, many people prefer to use hands-free cell phone equipment or send text messages, rather than holding the cell phone near their ear and brain.

Odd Magnetism and Supermagnets

The form of magnetism described so far in this book is called ferromagnetism because it is based on the metal iron (which has the scientific symbol Fe, short for the Latin word *ferrum*, meaning iron). This is not the only form of magnetism, however. There are other forms that scientists are studying, and that may become useful in the future.

More forms of magnetism

In diamagnetism, a substance exposed to a nearby magnetic field gains its own magnetism. But this magnetism repels it from a magnetic field. The metal bismuth shows this feature. This is the opposite of ferromagnetism, where the force is attraction. In paramagnetism, a substance that is not ferromagnetic is given magnetism by a nearby magnetic field, and is attracted to the strongest part of that field. Two strongly paramagnetic substances are the rare metals platinum and palladium.

High-power magnets

Very powerful and specialized magnets are used in many kinds of scientific research, and some of these ideas could be used in everyday life in the future. Almost any substance can be made to respond to magnetism of some kind— even a frog! In one experiment, a frog was subjected to such a powerful magnetic field that it became a magnet itself, and it was made to float by magnetic repulsion.

This type of scientific research may well sound strange, but it might lead to undreamed-of uses for magnetism.

Famous frog!
This frog has been magnetized and is floating as a result of a form of maglev called magnetic repulsion; it may be a bit surprised, but it was not hurt!

In nuclear power plants, electricity is made from the energy released when the centers of atoms split apart. This process is called nuclear fission. However, the process produces dangerous radioactivity. Another choice may be nuclear fusion, where parts of atoms are joined. This would produce much less radioactivity. However, to make fusion happen, a temperature of 212 million °F (100 million °C) are needed—far hotter than the Sun. No physical object can touch a substance at this temperature. It can only be contained by incredibly powerful magnetic fields from electromagnets. Scientists continue to study fusion power as a source of energy for the future.

Magnets in the future

One area of active research today is into producing superconductor materials for wires, which could carry electricity much more effectively than the materials now used for this. This would allow electromagnets to make a much more powerful magnetic field and would save huge amounts of energy and natural resources. In medicine, new techniques might use magnetism from superconductor electromagnets to heal disease and relieve pain. Magnetism would also allow maglev trains (see page 16) to run using much less electricity for their electromagnets.

Superconductor
Superconductors carry electricity almost perfectly, far better than ordinary wires. Their magnetic fields easily make small objects levitate, or float.

The maglev idea might even be adapted to launch spacecraft! The craft would gain speed very rapidly by racing along a track powered by a line of superconducting electromagnets. It could be fired into space, almost like a bullet from a gun. One day there may even be antigravity devices that use magnetism, such as cars without wheels that float above the ground, or even a suit that is worn on the body so a person can fly.

The science of magnetism can be complicated. It involves things that are unfamiliar to most of us, such as magnetic flux, domains, solenoids, and electron spin. There are many features and processes to remember—not only the simple rule that like magnetic poles repel and unlike poles attract, but also ideas such as electromagnetic induction and the electromagnetic effect. Even expert scientists have a hard time explaining some of the more detailed aspects of magnetic fields and magnetic forces. Also, magnetism itself is invisible. Often it is difficult to understand what we cannot see.

The units that measure magnetism are also unfamiliar. We become familiar with units such as feet or meters for length and ounces or grams for weight, when we can see what we are measuring. Magnetic units such as teslas and webers are much harder to understand, especially because we cannot see the magnetism they are measuring. Yet these units are important to designers and engineers in many areas of science and technology.

Magnets on the Moon
When astronauts landed on the Moon, from 1969 to 1972, they took experiments to study magnetism in space and on other worlds.

Yet magnets and magnetism are all around us—from Earth's magnetic field, to the hundreds of magnets and electromagnets we use in everyday life. When we turn on any electric-powered machine, turn on the television, listen to music from a sound system or radio, use a vehicle central locking system, or shut a cupboard door with a magnetic catch, we use magnetism. Often the magnetism is combined with its twin, electricity, as electromagnetic force—one of the most important forces in the whole universe.

Glossary

alternating current (AC) flow of electricity that changes direction, usually many times per second

atom tiniest particle of a pure substance, which is itself made up of smaller or subatomic particles

commutator part of an electric motor that reverses the direction of electrical flow to the wire coils as the motor spins

core in an electromagnet, the bar or rod (usually iron) placed in the solenoid (coil of wire)

declination difference in angle between the direction a compass needle points to, and true magnetic north, where it should point

diaphragm thin sheet that can vibrate easily, used in microphones and loudspeakers

digital working in small separate steps or stages

direct current (DC) flow of electricity in one direction only

domains tiny areas of magnetism that make up a larger magnet

electric charge a type of force, either positive or negative, possessed by particles in an atom, especially protons (+) and electrons (–)

electromagnet device that produces magnetism from flowing electricity, where the magnetism disappears when the electricity is switched off

electromagnetic effect producing magnetism using electricity

electromagnetic force combined electrical and magnetic energy

electromagnetic induction producing electricity using magnetism

electrons subatomic particles with a negative charge

ferrous metal metallic substance made of or containing iron

force push or pull that causes a change in movement or shape

generator device that changes movement energy into electricity

hard in magnetism, a word that describes a substance made into a magnet that keeps its magnetism for a long time

inclination angle at which Earth's invisible lines of magnetic force enter the ground

induction motor motor that uses alternating current (AC)

maglev magnetic levitation, the use of magnetism to lift (levitate) or move objects

magnetic field area around a magnet where the magnetic effect extends

magnetic flux broadly, strength or amount of magnetism

magnetic force push or pull exerted on magnetic material by a magnet

magnetic induction production by a magnet of another magnetic field in a nearby object

magnetic medium substance that retains tiny patches of magnetism and is used to store information in magnetic form

motor usual name for electric motor, which turns electricity into the energy of movement using magnetic forces

neutron subatomic particle with no charge, found in the nucleus of an atom

nuclear fission reaction in which the nucleus of an atom splits into various parts, releasing energy

nuclear fusion reaction in which two small, light nuclei fuse together to form a single heavier nucleus, releasing energy

nucleus central part of an atom, containing protons and neutrons

permanent magnet magnet that retains its magnetic force all the time

pole in magnetism, one of the two places on a magnet where the magnetic force is strongest

proton positively charged subatomic particle found in the nucleus of an atom

retentivity ability of a substance to retain its magnetic field over a long period

rotor in a generator or electric motor, a coil of wire or group of coils that rotate

soft in magnetism, word that describes a substance made into a magnet by another magnetic field that loses its magnetism when the other field is removed

solenoid wire wound into a long coil, as used in electromagnets

static electricity electrical charge that builds up on a object as electrons are either rubbed off or deposited on to it

stator in a generator or electric motor, a coil of wire or group of coils that stay still and do not rotate

subatomic particles particles smaller than an atom, such as the electrons, protons, and neutrons, that make up atoms

tesla unit of magnetic flux density, used to measure the amount of magnetism (magnetic flux) in a certain area, 1 tesla = 1 weber per square meter (see **weber**)

transformer device that changes the voltage in an electrical system

volt unit for measuring the strength, or push, of electricity (potential difference)

voltage the strength, or push, of electricity (potential difference)

weber unit of magnetic flux, or amount of magnetism, for example, used to measure the strength of the whole magnetic field around a magnet (see **tesla**)

Further Reading

Books

Carmi, Rebecca. *Amazing Magnetism.* New York: Scholastic, 2002.

Cooper, Christopher. *Science Answers: Magnetism from Pole to Pole.* Chicago: Heinemann Library, 2003.

The Dorling Kindersley Science Encyclopedia. New York: Dorling Kindersley, 1999.

Hewitt, Sally and Catherine Ward. *Fascinating Science Projects: Electricity and Magnetism.* New York: Franklin Watts, 2002.

Oxlade, Chris. *Science Topics: Electricity and Magnetism.* Chicago: Heinemann Library, 1999.

Taylor, Barbara. *Focus on Science: Electricity and Magnetism.* New York: Franklin Watts, 2003.

Index

Lizards

John Coborn

Published in association with T.F.H. Publications, Inc.,
the world's largest and most respected publisher of pet literature

Chelsea House Publishers
Philadelphia

Contents

Basic Domestic Reptile and Amphibian Library

Box Turtles
Lizards
Green Iguanas and Other Igaunids
Reptile and Amphibian Parasites
Newts
Snakes
Tarantulas and Scorpions
Chameleons
Tortoises

Publisher's Note: All of the photographs in this book have been coated with FOTOGLAZE™ finish, a special lamination that imparts a new dimension of colorful gloss to the photographs.

Reinforced Library binding & Super-Highest Quality Boards

This edition ©1999 Chelsea House Publishers, a division of Main Line Book Company.

Library of Congress Cataloging-in-Publication Data applied for 0-7910-5084-X

Library of Congress Cataloging-in-Publication Data

Coborn, John.
     Lizards / John Coborn.
     p.   cm. — (Reptiles and amphibians)
     Includes index.
     Summary: Discusses the natural history, selection, care, and breeding of lizards, including those who like to climb and those who live in deserts.
     ISBN 0-7910-5084-X (hc)
     1. Lizards as pets—Juvenile literature.   2. Lizards—Juvenile literature.
     [1. Lizards as pets.   2. Pets.]   I. Title. II. Series.
     SF459.L5C624 1998
     639.3'95—dc21
                                                98-22377
                                              CIP
                                              AC

LIZARDS FOR BEGINNERS

PREFACE

I have had an almost fanatical interest in lizards ever since I was a small child. Pictures of exotic species conjured up visions of giant dinosaurs roaming the plains or of ferocious dragons on the hunt for human prey. Most modern lizards, however, are totally harmless to human beings, and none of them really go out of their way to eat us!

Green Anoles, *Anolis carolinensis,* are small and hardy insectivores. One would make an excellent first pet lizard. Photo by Isabelle Francais

As a child I captured and kept the little common lizards, *Lacerta vivipara,* of my native England and was fascinated by their apparently endless appetite as they devoured the numerous little spiders and insects I fed to them. Later I graduated to more exotic species from southern Europe, Africa, and North America, many of which could be obtained in pet shops or from specialist importers. Eventually I became a reptile curator in a zoological park, where I gained experience with a great number of species from many parts of the world.

During the past couple of decades those who practice lizard keeping as a hobby have increased dramatically in numbers. New enthusiasts are continually joining the hobby, and there is an escalating quest for new facts about the biology and care of these fascinating reptiles. Students of zoology are increasingly turning to herpetology in their curricula, and studies on the ecology and behavior of lizards in the wild are producing many interesting and astonishing facts. At the same time, while taxonomists continue to revise the classification of known species, new species are still being discovered and described sporadically. Indeed, a new species of skink, which has even been relegated to a new genus, recently was discovered just 40 miles away from my home in Australia.

This work is intended to be a small but concise guide to lizard keeping as a hobby, and I have endeavored to include all of the information that the beginner to lizard keeping will require to set him off on the right footing for a long and fascinating affair with these charming creatures.

SOME LIZARD NATURAL HISTORY

Lizards form the zoological suborder Lacertilia and share with snakes (suborder Serpentes) the order Squamata, which is contained in the class Reptilia. Being reptiles, lizards have characteristics that make them different from other classes of vertebrates such as fishes, amphibians, birds, and mammals. Some typical characteristics of reptiles are that they have a dry, scaly skin; respire with lungs; and are ectothermic (cold-blooded). No other class of vertebrate (backboned) animals has all of these attributes. Fish may have scales and be ectothermic, but they don't have lungs. Amphibians may be ectothermic and have lungs, but they don't have a scaly skin; while birds and mammals both are endothermic (warm-blooded).

Different species of lizards form more than one half of the total species of recent reptiles, and over 3,700 species are recognized. They range in size from the tiny, rare Virgin Gorda Gecko, *Sphaerodactylus parthenopion*, which reaches a maximum length (including tail) of 3.8 cm (1.5 in), to the massive Komodo Dragon,

Amblyrhynchus cristatus, the Marine Iguana, lives in colonies on the Galapagos Islands. They are legally protected and never available to the hobbyist. Photo by Karl H. Switak

Smile! Not really. This is the defensive display of a Tokay Gecko, *Gekko gecko.*Photo by Karl H. Switak

Varanus komodoensis, with a recorded length of 3.1 m (10 ft 2 in). This record specimen was exhibited in the St. Louis Zoological Gardens, Missouri, during 1937, at which time it weighed 166 kg (365 lb)! The vast majority of lizard species, however, are confined to a length range of 15-45 cm (6-18 in).

Lizards occur in suitable climates on every continent except Antarctica. They are found in habitats ranging from deserts to rainforests, and from prairies to mountain ranges. Although the greatest number of species occur in the tropics and subtropics, some are found as far north as southern Canada and as far south as Tierra del Fuego at the tip of South America. In Europe, the Viviparous Lizard, *Lacerta vivipara*, extends to some areas within the Arctic Circle. A few species are littoral (inhabiting the seashore), while others are semiaquatic in freshwater. A single species, the Marine Iguana, *Amblyrhynchus cristatus*, of the Galapagos Islands, actually forages below sea level for its staple diet of seaweed!

A typical lizard has an elongated body and a long, tapering tail. It has four limbs, each furnished with five digits. However, there are many variations from the typical; some have reductions in the number of digits, others have reduced or vestigial limbs or even no visible limbs at all. There are other species with short fat tails instead of long tapering ones.

One distinctive feature of lizards and other reptiles is the horny skin that is folded into

Another typical feature of many lizard species is the ability to shed all or part of the tail. Some shed the tail readily and voluntarily, others less readily only when the tail is seized by a predator. The tail is shed by a process known as autotomy, and the break occurs across a weak spot (the fracture plane) across one of the tail

This male South American anole, *Anolis fuscoauratus*, has extended his brightly colored dewlap. This indicates he is defending his territory or wooing a potential mate.Photo by Paul Freed

scales. Different species have varying types of scales; some are large and plate-like, others are tiny and granular. Scales may overlap or may be juxtaposed. They may be smooth and glossy in some species, rough and keeled in others. In some lizards, many of the scales are modified into protective spines.

vertebrae. Tail shedding is a protective mechanism that keeps a predator occupied with the wriggling appendage while the main body of the animal quickly makes its escape. A new but less spectacular tail will eventually grow in place of the shed one. Another feature of the tail in some lizards, especially chamaeleons

The Veiled Chameleon, *Chamaeleo calyptratus*, is a beautiful but demanding captive. Photo by Zoltan Takacs

and Prehensile-tailed Skinks, *Corucia zebrata*, is prehensility. The tail, in effect, acts as a fifth limb, allowing the reptiles to grip twigs and branches and giving them more stability.

While most lizards are carnivorous (meat eaters), preying on invertebrate and vertebrate animals of suitable size, some are omnivorous, feeding on a mixture of animal and vegetable foods, and a few are quite herbivorous, feeding mostly on vegetation.

An important reptilian feature of lizards that has a bearing on the way we keep them is the fact that they are ectothermic or cold-blooded. This means that unlike birds and mammals, lizards are unable to maintain a constant optimum body temperature through metabolism; they have to rely on external temperatures through a process known as behavioral thermoregulation. In the morning a lizard will emerge from its overnight refuge and bask in the sun until it reaches an optimum operating temperature. It then goes off to seek food or indulge in mating activities before seeking out a shady, cooler spot where it can cool down somewhat. By moving from warmer to cooler spots throughout the day, the lizard can maintain a surprisingly constant temperature. It instinctively knows its optimum temperature requirement and actively regulates it. In cooler temperate regions, lizards remain inactive, often through several months of hibernation, until temperatures are again high enough for them to function efficiently. It is only in tropical areas that lizards may be active throughout the year, and even there they may enter into estivation during periods of drought. It is in tropical regions that the majority of nocturnal lizards live, especially geckos.

A close-up view of the beautiful dorsal crest of a male Green Basilisk, *Basiliscus plumifrons*. In the female, the crest is greatly reduced. Photo by David J. Zoffer

HOUSING FOR PET LIZARDS

The type of housing you will use for your pet lizards will depend on the size of the species you intend to keep and its ecological requirements. You should always have the accommodations ready to use before you acquire any lizards. It is a mistake to obtain specimens first and then have to worry about how you are going to house them. In this and the following chapter we will be discussing types of housing for pet lizards and the life support systems that will provide the correct environmental requirements for a range of species.

THE GLASS TERRARIUM

A simple glass aquarium tank of the type sold for fish keeping is ideal as a starter terrarium and can be used for many species. Most modern aquarium tanks are constructed from glass sheets cemented together with special silicone adhesive. Such aquaria can be purchased at any pet shop and come in various sizes. You can have a terrarium constructed to order, specifying the shape and dimensions of the tank to your own special needs (perhaps you have some corner or alcove in the house where you need a terrarium of specific design) and to the

A Collared Lizard, *Crotaphytus collaris.* This species requires a large, arid terrarium to thrive. Photo by Aaron Norman

This juvenile Nile Monitor, *Varanus niloticus,* can grow to a length of 6 feet or more. Its size and aggressive disposition make this a poor choice for the beginner.Photo by R. D. Bartlett

needs of the species you are going to keep. Terrestrial lizards, for example, will need a relatively low, flat construction with a large floor area, while arboreal species require a tall tank with room to affix vertical branches and tall plants.

The lid of the terrarium can be made from a piece of thick, heavy plywood or sheet aluminum with two large holes (one at each end) covered with fine wire gauze, for ventilation purposes. Cut the lid to size so that it just rests on the strengthening strips just inside the top of the tank. A small handle affixed to the lid will make it easy to lift off when necessary. As many lizard species are talented escape artists, ensure that there are no gaps wider than 3 mm (0.12 in). A much simpler

and usually satisfactory alternative is to purchase a standard lid at your pet shop. These usually consist of a metal or plastic frame fitted with mesh or wire screening of various sizes. In some lids the screened portion is attached so it can be slid out rather than lifted off, an excellent way to help prevent escapes.

Terraria can, of course, be constructed from a range of other materials, including wood, metal, fiberglass, and so on. I have seen some excellent lizard cages improvised from such items as old TV cabinets and shop display cabinets. Many specialist dealers today make custom terraria that range from large rainforest enclosures complete with humidifiers to shelf units designed to hold the shoe boxes

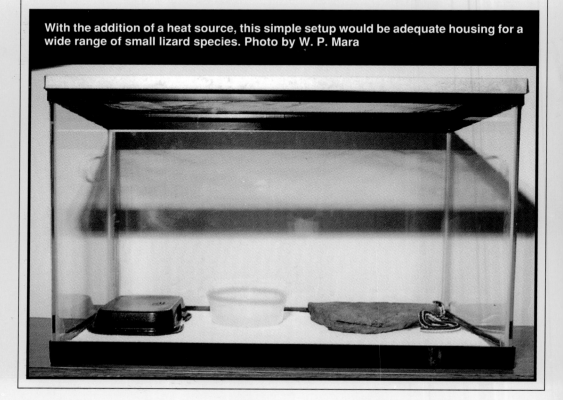

With the addition of a heat source, this simple setup would be adequate housing for a wide range of small lizard species. Photo by W. P. Mara

This outdoor enclosure with live plants is ideal for arboreal lizards such as chameleons and day geckos. Photo by R. D. Bartlett.

and sweater boxes in which many lizards are bred commercially. The main requirements are that terraria must be escape-proof and able to resist humidity in the case of rainforest displays. When using wood, it is best to preserve it with a coating of water-resistant varnish, paint, or fiberglass resin, being sure that all residues and volatile components have plenty of time to totally disperse.

CAGE FURNISHINGS

Substrate Materials

Simple breeding or rearing cages are best floored with newspaper or paper towels. These are absorbent and easy to change frequently. For the display terrarium a substrate of gravel, leaf litter, bark chippings, or similar materials is suitable. A recent innovation is terrarium carpeting, a floor covering produced by several companies. Such floor coverings are attractive, mildew resistant, and washable. Less suitable substitutes include synthetic grass carpeting or even old bath towels. Whatever kind of flooring is used, it is important that it is cleaned and sterilized regularly. It is a good idea to have spare floor coverings ready to replace those that are being cleaned.

Rocks

These provide a natural looking backdrop for species from desert

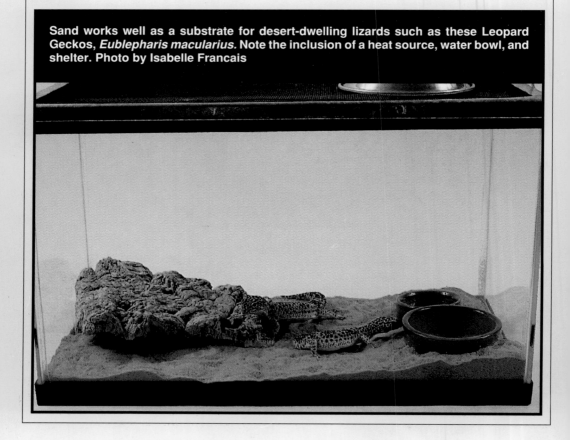

Sand works well as a substrate for desert-dwelling lizards such as these Leopard Geckos, *Eublepharis macularius.* Note the inclusion of a heat source, water bowl, and shelter. Photo by Isabelle Francais

An artificial cow skull, cactus, and cholla wood enrich this Leopard Gecko enclosure. Photo by Jerry R. Loll

or rocky areas and will supply locations on which they can bask. You can purchase suitable rocks in pet shops, including those made of Styrofoam or papier mache to reduce weight. Rocks can be piled up to create caves and crevices that your lizards will use as refuges, but be sure they are fixed securely to avoid accidents; silicone cements work well. You can collect your own rocks, but be sure they are thoroughly cleaned and dried before you use them.

Tree Branches

Climbing lizards will require branches and twigs on which to practice their skills, as well as to bask. Dead wood is preferable to branches recently cut from living trees, some of which may emit poisonous saps. Driftwood from river banks or from the sea shore is ideal as it will have been exposed to the elements, will be attractively sun bleached, and usually is relatively smooth; be sure to thoroughly soak all driftwood to remove salt, silt, and dead plants and animals. Branches should be fixed securely in the cage so that they are unable to topple. A climbing branch that ends directly at the surface of the terrarium might be an excellent escape route for an active lizard, so it might be best to be sure all branches are fixed at least a few centimeters below the rim.

Plants

There is no doubt that a display of healthy plants in the terrarium adds an esthetic charm that is hard to beat. Rainforest terraria in particular should have a few living plants. It is best to retain living plants in their pots. These can be arranged in the terrarium and the pots concealed with rocks or bits of cork bark. Many plant species of the type commonly marketed as "house plants" are suitable for the humid terrarium. Cacti and succulents may be suitable for drier terraria. It always is best to keep a spare set of plants so that you can change them at intervals while the stressed plants relax in sunshine for a month or so. Unfortunately, there is not much point in trying to grow plants along with large, boisterous lizards, especially herbivorous species. In such cases artificial plants can be used effectively.

This Koch's Day Gecko, *Phelsuma madagascariensis kochi,* basks on a bamboo perch. This arboreal species fares well in a tall, well-planted terrarium. Photo by R. D. Bartlett.

LIFE SUPPORT SYSTEMS

Lizards kept in captivity must be provided with environmental conditions that are as near as possible to those of their native habitats. As it usually is impossible to mimic natural conditions in the enclosed terrarium, we have to use compromise systems in order to reproduce an optimum environment.

TEMPERATURE

Being ectothermic (cold-blooded), lizards are unable to maintain their body temperatures at a relatively constant level without the assistance of an external heat source. In nature, the natural heat sources mainly come directly or indirectly from the sun. By the process of thermoregulation, lizards

Access to the proper range of temperatures is essential to successful lizard keeping. This Australian skink, *Egernia hosmeri,* prefers temperatures between 80 and 100 degrees Fahrenheit. Photo by R. W. VanDevender

The climatic constituents that we have to take into consideration are temperature, lighting and photoperiod, ventilation, and humidity. Modern technology now enables us to produce optimum conditions for habitats ranging from arid deserts to tropical rain forests.

maintain an optimum body temperature by basking directly in the sun and/or by coming into contact with sun-warmed surfaces. Unless we keep our lizards in open-air enclosures, it is usually quite impossible to use natural sunlight as a source of heat. Sunlight through the glass of a terrarium will be magnified, and the terrarium will overheat dramatically in a short space of time. Many a novice lizard keeper has lost his pets through placing their terrarium in direct sunlight. Electrical heating of one form or another is the answer to this problem.

Incandescent Bulbs

The simplest method of terrarium heating, and one that has been in use since the pioneering days of terrarium keeping, is the ordinary domestic incandescent (tungsten) light bulb. Bulbs come in various sizes (wattages), and one or more can be used to maintain suitable temperatures in terraria of most sizes. Unfortunately the quality of light emitted by such bulbs is inadequate for the requirements of most diurnal basking lizards, so they must be used in conjunction with other light sources. Recently some manufacturers have produced specially coated bulbs that mimic at least some of the wavelengths of light necessary for healthy lizards. Other special coatings provide heat with little or no light, useful when warming nocturnally active lizards. A bulb used for heating can be installed in the terrarium lid, and the required temperature can be maintained by experimenting with a thermometer and various wattages, or by use of a thermostat. It usually is prudent to mount the bulb in a socket that is contained within a reflective shade so that most of the heat is directed onto a basking surface below the lamp. The temperature of the basking area can be adjusted by raising or lowering the lamp.

Because all incandescent bulbs can cause horrendous burns if a lizard should gain access to them, all bulbs must be securely mounted above the terrarium lid with strong screening below so no lizard can get close to them.

A more up to date version of the tungsten bulb is the spotlight that has its own built-in reflector. They can be used in much the same way as the normal bulbs. Infra-red bulbs that emit either white or red light also often are used specifically to warm up basking areas. A disadvantage of light-emitting bulbs used for heating is that they emit light continuously, even at night when it is not required. This can be overcome to some extent by using a dark colored (red or blue) bulb at night. As the night temperature usually must be cooler than that of the day, the colored bulb should be of a lower wattage than the day bulb. For example, a 100 watt bulb normally will provide adequate daytime heating for a small terrarium with dimensions of 60 x 30 x 30 cm (approx. 24 x 12 x 12 in) and a 25 watt colored bulb will suffice for the night.

Heating Pads, Tapes, and Cables

A number of electrical heating devices specially manufactured for terraria are available. Heating pads may be placed below terraria or can be used against one of the sides. Cables may be useful for placing in a gravel substrate, while tapes can be affixed along the bottom edges of the terrarium. Heating tapes usually require that they be cut to fit the terrarium and then wired into the main circuits; if you are unsure as to how to set up tapes, for safety consult an electrician.

devices should be used specifically to the manufacturer's instructions. They must never get wet while plugged in, should always be kept clean, and must be carefully watched for hot spots. In the case of lizards that thermoregulate by basking in sunlight from above (Green

Banded geckos, like this *Coleonyx mitratus* hatchling, are occasionally offered for sale. They need a hot and fairly dry environment. Photo by R. D. Bartlett

Heated Rocks

The most recent special heating innovations for terraria are so called "hot rocks," artificial pieces of rock (usually made from plaster of Paris or a plastic resin) containing a heating element that may or may not be controlled thermostatically. Needless to say, the thermostatically controlled rocks are more efficient. All commercially produced heating

Iguanas, etc.), the pineal eye on top of the skull keeps track of how much basking time is necessary for the lizard; heat from below, especially directly against the belly, may not register and the lizard may not be able to sense the fact that it is burning. Hot rocks have led to bad ventral burns in some lizards when not accompanied by overhead basking lights.

Veiled Chameleons, *Chamaeleo calyptratus*, need to be kept in cages that are warm, moist, and furnished with plenty of climbing branches. This is a gravid female. Photo by R. D. Bartlett

Aquarium Heaters

Tubular glass aquarium heaters, with or without a thermostat, may have their uses in the lizard terrarium, especially for species that need high humidity. In the aquaterrarium, the aquarium heater simply can be placed in the water area and used just as you would use it in an aquarium for tropical fish. Alternatively, where a large body of water is not required, the aquarium heater can be placed in a tall jar of water that can be concealed in a corner of the terrarium. The heater cable should be passed through a perforated lid fixed over the jar to prevent lizards from gaining access and accidentally drowning. Some aquarium heaters can be used out of water and can be placed inside a hollowed out log, a clay pipe, or an artificial hollow rock. Most common aquarium heaters, however, will malfunction if turned on when dry.

Temperature Gradation

As lizards have a preferred optimum temperature, it is dangerous to expose them to a constant high temperature without facilities to cool off. A temperature gradation in the terrarium will allow the reptiles to move from warmer to cooler parts of the substrate and vice versa. This can be achieved by placing the heating apparatus at only one end of the terrarium. The main basking area will be close to the heat source, temperatures becoming progressively less toward the other end of the cage. When using a thermostat it is best to place the sensor in the center of the terrarium and set it to an average temperature. If, for example, you want the temperature to be 30°C (86°F) at the "hot" end and 24°C (75°F) at the cold end, you could try setting the thermostat at 27°C (81°F). You may have to experiment using a thermometer before you get it right.

Night Temperature

Night temperatures often are lower than those prevailing during the day. The differences between day and night temperatures may be as much as 15°C (about 30°F) for species from temperate, subtropical, and tropical montane regions to as little as 4°C (about 8°F) for species from lowland equatorial regions. For many species the heating apparatus can be simply switched off at night; the room temperature in most dwellings is adequate overnight. Should higher nighttime temperatures be required, it may be necessary to have a double thermostat system, one for daytime, the other for nighttime.

Seasonal Temperature

Seasonal temperature changes should also be provided where necessary. Species from temperate and subtropical regions are especially influenced by seasonal temperature changes as well as photoperiod. While winter temperatures in some natural habitats may descend to below the freezing point, lizards from such areas know where to hibernate to avoid sub-zero temperatures. (Of course, the terrarium would have to provide sufficiently deep substrates to allow them to burrow to a warm level.) It would be dangerous in the terrarium to copy such winter climates, and a compromise reduction of temperature for a shorter period is adequate. A winter reduction of 10°C (about 20°F) usually is satisfactory.

LIGHTING

Lighting goes hand in hand with heating. Many lizard species require natural sunlight to remain in the best of health. The ultraviolet rays help stimulate the manufacture of essential vitamin D3, a deficiency that will cause various metabolic problems that could, over a period of time, even be fatal. Fortunately we now have forms of artificial lighting of a quality that is a good substitute for sunlight. Most such lights come in the form of fluorescent tubes that provide broad-spectrum lighting coming close to the necessary wavelengths of sunlight.

While incandescent bulbs used for heating will provide incidental supplementary light, they must be used in conjunction with broad-spectrum lamps for many diurnal basking species, especially those from temperate and subtropical regions.

Nocturnal lizards such as many geckos are less dependent on sunlight or its substitute, though it will do no harm to include broad-spectrum lighting in any setup.

Seasonal changes in photoperiod (hours of daylight) also are important, especially if we want our lizards to reproduce. We know that photoperiod decreases in the winter and increases in the summer. The seasonal changes in photoperiod are progressively greater from the Equator to the poles. In temperate regions the period of daylight can be as much as 16 hours in the summer and as little as eight hours in the winter. By knowing the latitude of your lizard species' natural habitat you will be able to work out the photoperiod requirements in the terrarium. Equatorial species of course require 12-hour photoperiods the year around, though even these may be stimulated to breed with a small reduction at the right time.

VENTILATION AND HUMIDITY

While adequate ventilation in the terrarium is important for the health of all species, humidity (air moisture level) requirements will vary from species to species depending on its habitat. Tropical rainforest species will require high humidity all year, while those from some subtropical or temperate areas will require variations in humidity depending on time of the year.

This is particularly important for species from those areas that experience pronounced wet and dry seasons. Species from arid and desert-like areas generally require low humidity throughout the year. The larger the water vessel in the terrarium, the greater the humidity will be, though heated and over-ventilated terraria tend to dry out very quickly. Desert-dwelling species should be provided with only a small dish of drinking water, as further humidity is not required. Conversely, rainforest and wet temperate forest species probably will require aids to maintaining high humidity. In addition to a large water vessel, you can spray regularly with a fine mist sprayer. An aquarium heater and an aerator in the water vessel will cause steady evaporation and its attendant high humidity. There are powered misting systems available for humidity-loving species. They tend to be expensive, but they can be helpful in keeping delicate chameleons, day geckos, and Monkey-tailed Skink healthy. In many situations it will be necessary to formulate a compromise situation between the ventilation and the humidity. Remember, however, that no lizards will thrive if they do not have access to dry surfaces.

This handsome lizard, *Agama minor,* is well suited for a naturalistic rocky terrarium. Photo by Aaron Norman.

FEEDING YOUR PETS

Lizards may be carnivorous, omnivorous, or mostly herbivorous, but the majority of species kept as pets fall into the first category. Most of the smaller lizards we keep will thrive on a variety of insects. Here the word variety is of utmost importance. As we know, all animals

Many lizards relish snails. The common garden snails, such as this *Helix aspersa,* are readily accepted "snacks." Photo by Ken Lucas

must have a balanced diet in order to keep in the best of health and to function properly. A balanced diet consists of macronutrients (proteins, fats, and carbohydrates) and so-called micronutrients (vitamins and minerals, many of which serve as catalysts to an animal's metabolism rather than true nutrients that are destroyed or modified during metabolism). Macronutrients form the bulk of a lizard's food, but the essential micronutrients are obtained through variety in the diet. You should ensure that you will have a continuing supply of the right types of food before you decide on what lizard species you wish to keep.

COLLECTING LIVE FOODS

While there are a number of excellent live food items that can

be purchased from pet shops or propagated at home, it is recommended that wild-collected live foods be offered when available. Many collected insects are far more nutritious than home-bred ones, and the use of these as a dietary supplement will go a long way toward introducing the required variety into the diet.

If you live in a big city it may not be possible to collect live foods on a regular basis. Also, there usually is a shortage of wild live foods during the winter months in colder areas. However, country dwellers will be able to collect live foods on a regular basis, while city-dwellers will have to limit their collecting trips to the occasional day in the country. An hour or so spent collecting insects during a summer outing can be very productive. Some backyards and gardens can also often reveal a surprising amount of invertebrate life. You will find that not all lizards will take all food items, but it is worth experimenting.

One of the best ways of collecting a variety of insects and spiders is to use a sweep net. This is like a butterfly net, but preferably with a canvas reinforced rim as it is quite likely to get a fair amount of wear and tear. You can sweep the net through tall grass and the foliage of shrubs and trees. In productive areas you soon will collect a variety of caterpillars, moths, beetles, grasshoppers, spiders, and so on. These can be size-graded and placed in small glass or plastic jars for transport home. In hot weather it is advisable to place a little foliage in the jars in order to maintain moisture.

Another good method of collecting is to look under rocks, logs, and other ground litter. Here you will find a variety of spiders, crickets, pillbugs, earthworms, slugs, snails, and so on. These can be collected and transported as described above. If you don't like to touch the insects, you can use a spoon to scoop them directly into a jar. By breaking open rotten timber or tearing off the bark, you may find a number

Spiders are common in many areas and add variety to the diets of insect-eating lizards. This is a species of sac spider in the genus *Castianeria*. Photo by Paul Freed

of insect grubs. In some areas you may be lucky enough to collect termites. The soft bodies of these "white ants" are a nutritious and readily accepted live food for many small insectivorous lizards.

Very small insects, for small or juvenile lizards, can be collected using a "pooter," which is a small plastic or glass jar with a suction tube fitted to it. This can be a cork with two holes, through each of which a plastic or metal tube passes. Two flexible rubber or plastic tubes are fitted over the tubes through the cork. The end of one of the flexible tubes is placed near the insects to be collected (often in the corolla of a flower where numerous small insects congregate), while the other is placed in the mouth. A sharp suck on the tube will cause the insects to be pulled into the jar. A piece of gauze placed over the mouth end will prevent you from getting an unwelcome meal!

RAISED LIVE FOODS

Over the past few years, the pet trade has shown an increasing interest in propagating several species of invertebrate foods especially for the welfare of captive insectivorous animals.

These are obtainable by quantity, weight, or volume, depending on the species. Some establishments sell by mail order, and others even sell cultures with instructions on how to further propagate them. You must decide for yourself whether you have the time and patience to cultivate your own live foods, or whether you want to buy small quantities on a regular basis. The following is a brief summary of some of the more commonly used live foods, with notes on their culture.

Crickets

These insects often are the main standby live food for insectivorous lizards. They are very nutritious and not difficult to breed. There are several species, but the best known is the common domestic cricket, *Acheta domesticus*. Adult crickets are about 2.5 cm (1 in) in length, while the hatchlings are about 3 mm (0.12 in), and there are several intermediate nymphal stages, giving a useful choice of sizes. Cricket cultures can be purchased quite easily. The insects are best kept in screened boxes or plastic bins furnished with old egg cartons or crumpled newspapers to act as hiding places. The crickets should be fed on a diet of cereal (bran, poultry meal, cornmeal, etc.) and a small amount of fresh vegetables daily (lettuce, carrot, apple, etc.). They will obtain most of their moisture from their food, but to be on the safe side it is advisable to provide them with a saucer or shallow dish containing a water-soaked sponge or cotton wadding (the insects will drown in open water)

Katydids are a nutritious food for lizards that are easy to find in the spring and summer. Small ones are common and giant ones can be found occasionally. Photo by M. Gilroy

Crickets form the bulk of many captive lizards' diets. Feed only as many crickets to your pet as it will eat at once; leftover crickets can get hungry enough to bite and injure a lizard.

so that they can drink if necessary. If maintained at a temperature around 26°C (79°F), the crickets will breed readily. The females may lay their eggs in a tray with moist sand or loose soil about 3 cm deep, and these normally hatch in about three weeks. It is best to remove the tray of eggs to a separate bin so that they are not eaten by the adults.

Mealworms

These have long been a standard live food for captive reptiles and birds. Relatively recent studies have shown that mealworms are not quite as nutritious as they might be due to an imbalance in their calcium to phosphorus ratio. However,

mealworms can still be considered an important part of a varied diet and can be nutritionally improved by adding a powdered vitamin/mineral supplement to their growing medium. Mealworms are the larvae of a flour beetle, *Tenebrio molitor*. They can be kept in shallow, screened boxes, with a 5-cm (2-in) layer of bran/oatmeal or bran/cornmeal mixture. A bit of fresh greens or vegetables placed daily on the surface of the growing medium will supply the larvae with adequate moisture. Though relatively slow-growing, mealworms will breed readily. Allow some of the worms to grow to full size and pupate. After a few weeks they will emerge as adult mealworm beetles (which in themselves are also acceptable to

Giant or King Mealworms are available at many pet stores. They are not as easy to culture as their smaller kin. Photo by David J. Zoffer.

many lizards). The beetles soon will mate and lay eggs that will hatch into tiny mealworms. The whole process takes place in the growing medium and, under favorable conditions, you should get a new generation every two to three months. They are best kept at a temperature of around 26°C (79°F). Be careful that humidity in the container does not increase to the point where fungus begins to grow in the culture.

Locusts

These are large grasshoppers that are serious agricultural pests in many parts of the world and, as such, have been subject to much scientific study. This means that many laboratories breed them in large numbers for experimental purposes and they frequently are available on the "pet food" market, at least in Europe; presently they

Many larger lizards readily devour locusts. This is an African variety. Photo by Mark Smith

It is easy to collect caterpillars in many areas. Some varieties can be ordered through biological supply companies. Photo by Mark Smith.

are uncommon foods in the United States. Like crickets, they are a nutritious form of live food for captive insectivorous lizards and, as the adults are relatively large (7.5 cm, 3 in), they are suitable for larger lizards. Like crickets, the nymphal stages come in various sizes. Locusts are kept in heated cages (an old aquarium is ideal) at about 28°C (82°F) and fed on oatmeal and grass stems. The stems are placed in a jar of water to keep them fresh and should be changed daily; pack cotton wadding around the mouth of the jar to keep the insects from drowning. Trays of just barely moist sand about 7.5 cm (3 in) deep should be provided for egg-laying.

Fuzzy mice are newborn mice that have only recently grown their fur. Many larger lizards such as monitors and tegus are fed mice exclusively.

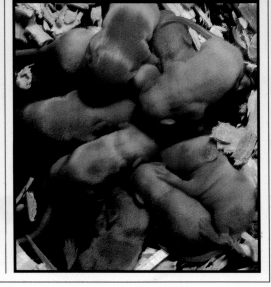

Silkworms

These have been bred intensively in the Orient for many generations and are the source of fine silk that is spun out of the cocoons made by the pupating larvae. Silkworms often are used in school biology classes and are fairly obtainable. The silkworms are the caterpillars of the silk moth, and both the larvae and the adult moths are useful as food for many lizards. The caterpillars feed on the foliage of mulberry trees. Leafy twigs from the tree can be placed in a jar of water to keep

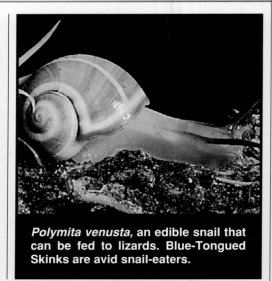

Polymita venusta, an edible snail that can be fed to lizards. Blue-Tongued Skinks are avid snail-eaters.

A variety of mixed vegetables and fruits can be offered daily to herbivorous lizards. Photo by Isabelle Francais

them fresh and placed in a screened cage. Net material wrapped around a wire frame will confine your culture admirably. Replace the mulberry twigs as necessary.

Fruitflies

These are essential if you are raising small juvenile lizards. They also are accepted by some of the smaller species of adult lizards. In summer you usually can collect fruitflies by putting a box of banana skins or rotting fruit in a remote corner of the garden. As the flies accumulate you can whisk them up in a fine-meshed net. You also may be able to obtain a fruitfly culture, plus instructions and culture media, from a specialist supplier advertising in reptile magazines.

Vertebrate Foods

Mice, rats, chickens, pigeons, quail, and so on often are used as food for some of the larger lizards, especially monitors, large agamids, and some iguanas. Pinkie mice (juveniles that have not yet developed fur) are very useful food items for many smaller lizards. You can purchase supplies of vertebrate food items from many pet shops, where they are sold both living and frozen. Some companies specialize in killed, frozen mice, rats, and chicks. These should be thoroughly thawed out before being fed to your pets. In general it is better to feed such items to lizards rather than using strips of chicken or beef meat that do not

constitute a balanced diet. Pinkies and other vertebrate foods contain a large amount of calcium (from the skeleton).

VEGETABLE FOODS

Herbivorous and omnivorous lizards require a variety of vegetable foods. While green food such as lettuce may be taken eagerly by some lizards, this is not very nutritious and should be only a small part of a diet containing various fruits, vegetables, buds, and flowers. Give your lizards a mixture of chopped items and see what they prefer to eat. This will allow you to develop a feeding strategy.

Whatever the diet of your lizards, it should be regularly supplemented with a good vitamin/mineral preparation. Powdered preparations can be sprinkled over the food before you give it to the lizards. A supplement about twice per week should be adequate.

FREQUENCY OF FEEDING

It is difficult to lay down any hard and fast rules regarding how often you feed your lizards. In general it can be said that juvenile lizards and small species should be fed daily. This also applies to species that are largely herbivorous. Two or three sizable meals per week are usually adequate for large carnivorous lizards. Beware not to overfeed your lizards; this will lead to obesity and associated problems. It is better to err on the "too little" rather than on the "too much" side.

CARING FOR SICK LIZARDS

As long as your pet lizards are given optimum conditions in which to live and are provided with a suitable balanced diet, they are unlikely to get sick. Indeed, most cases of sickness are often directly or indirectly related to poor husbandry. In the past, when we knew much less about captive reptile welfare, many lizards were lost within a few weeks of their acquisition because of ignorance on the part of the keeper.

The proper way to hold small lizards. With the lizard held firmly, its health can be assessed and proper care administered. Photo by W. P. Mara

PREVENTION IS BETTER THAN CURE

It is much better to know the causes of ill health and to prevent sickness rather than having to worry about curing an outbreak of disease when it happens. The provision of correct environmental conditions and provision of a proper diet will go a long way toward keeping our lizards healthy. Lizards kept in unsuitable conditions will suffer stress, their natural immunities will diminish, and they will be open to infection.

General Hygiene

It should go without saying that cages must be kept as clean as possible. Feces must be removed daily and fresh water should always be available. Cages and furnishings should be stripped down and cleaned at regular intervals. This will include scrubbing the interior of the cage and the furnishings with a weak solution of household bleach and thoroughly rinsing off with warm water and drying out before the lizards are replaced. Try and keep the furnishing arrangements fairly constant; lizards tend to get to know well what they regard as their territory and will be confused if you make changes every time you clean out the cage. Personal hygiene is also important. Keep an old set of clothes to wear when servicing your terraria. Always wash your hands before moving from one terrarium to the next.

Handling

Most lizards prefer not to be handled, though there are a few species that don't seem to mind too much. Most of the more commonly kept pet lizards will become accustomed to being handled on a regular basis as long as you are quiet and gentle in your actions. In the case of small, delicate, or nervous lizards such as anoles and geckos it is best not to handle them at all unless strictly necessary. It is much better to admire them by sight only, rather than to risk stressing them by too much handling. Lizards that are handled too much are much less likely to breed than those that are left undisturbed.

Small lizards up to about 15 cm (6 in) in length can be cupped in the hands and examined by opening the fingers. Some of the more lively little characters can be difficult to restrain without injuring them, so you may require some practice. Most lizards will attempt to bite if they are unused to handling, but those in the small range are incapable of giving more than a little nip that is unlikely to break the skin.

Medium sized lizards, from 15 cm (6 in) to about 45 cm (18 in), should be grasped around the thorax gently but firmly while restraining the head with the thumb and forefinger to prevent biting. Some lizards in this group are capable of giving a fairly powerful and painful bite, and sometimes the skin will be broken. Accidental bites should be swabbed with an antiseptic solution and covered with small bandages to them clean.

The range of good nutritional and health care products available to keepers of reptiles and amphibians continues to grow as professionals in the field expand their knowledge of herps' needs. Photo: Courtesy of Mardel Laboratories, Inc.

Water bowls must be kept clean to prevent disease. A solution of bleach and soapy water will safely disinfect them. Rinse well. Photo by Isabelle Francais

However, a practiced lizard keeper should be able to easily handle his lizards without getting bitten.

Large lizards from about 45 cm (18 in) to 1 m (40 in) or more are not recommended for beginners. Most large iguanas and monitors, unless they are hand-tame, will bite and scratch fiercely if given the chance. They should be grasped firmly around the neck with one hand and lifted bodily with the other hand. The tail and hindlimbs can be restrained by tucking them under the elbow. Bites and scratches from large lizards can cause severe lacerations that may require medical attention, so be careful!

Acquiring Pet Lizards

Most pet lizards today are purchased from pet shops, specialist dealers, or breeders. The days of collecting specimens from the wild are almost over, as most of the popular pet species are protected in Northern Hemisphere countries, and personal importation of "pets" collected or bought during that vacation to the tropics has become more complicated. One time you will need to handle lizards is when you give them their pre-purchase inspection. This will be necessary because you want to be sure that the lizards are healthy from the outset. Examine your prospective purchases carefully. Do not buy from dealers with dirty or overcrowded cages. Do not buy emaciated lizards even if you think you can save them. Tell-tale signs of sick or malnourished lizards are sunken eyes, lethargy, hollow abdomens, dull, loose skin, and hollows at the tail base. Make sure the eyes are bright and clear; that the mouth and the vent are clean and uninfected; and that the skin is unbroken and unblemished. Inspect the joints and digits for signs of articular gout (lameness and/or hard lumps in the joints) and ensure that the animal is alert and lively.

Taking Them Home

Once you have purchased your stock, you must try and get it home and into its new quarters as soon as possible. Lizards usually are transported in soft cloth bags that are tied at the top with a

Children must be taught to wash their hands after handling reptiles to prevent a *Salmonella* infection. Supervision is essential. Photo by Isabelle Francais

knot or tape. Each lizard preferably should be placed in its own bag and the bags placed in a cardboard box. Don't leave your lizards in situations where they will get too cold or too hot; many a lizard in its bag has been lost by leaving it in a cold car overnight or in hot sun during the day.

QUARANTINE

If you have just acquired your first lizards you can place them directly into their newly prepared home. However, if you already have lizards and you have acquired additional specimens, it is important to keep them in isolation for a period of three weeks or more before introducing them to any of your existing stock. This period of quarantine is to ensure that your new lizards are not sickening from any infectious disease that could

infect all of your stock. Even though you may have been very vigilant in your initial health inspection, there is a small chance that you may have missed something or that an animal is infected in its early stages and not yet showing any symptoms. A quarantine cage should be placed in a room separate from your main collection. It should be simply furnished but have all of the necessary life-support systems. If quarantined lizards show no signs of disease after three weeks, it usually is safe to house them in their more permanent quarters.

DISEASES AND TREATMENTS

Although we will have tried our utmost to prevent outbreaks of

Even this feisty Tokay Gecko should be quarantined before introduction into an established collection. Photo by Karl H. Switak

disease, unfortunate incidents may happen from time to time. Many veterinarians recently have been turning their attentions to some of the more exotic kinds of pets, and there are those who specialize in reptiles. Though your local veterinarian may not be an expert on lizards, he will most likely be able to communicate with one who is knowledgeable. Lizards are valuable and deserve the best of treatment. Whenever in doubt about the health of your pets, please be sure to obtain the appropriate veterinary advice rather than take do-it-yourself measures. The following is a brief summary of the more common diseases and conditions of captive lizards.

Towels are useful for restraining defensive lizards during any necessary handling. This is *Corucia zebrata*, the Prehensile-tailed Skink Photo by Karl H. Switak.

and broken bones will require treatment and possibly surgery by your veterinarian.

Nutritional Diseases
These occur as a result of an inadequate diet and should not happen if you feed your animals properly. Most of the conditions arise as the result of a deficiency in various vitamins or minerals due to insufficient variety in the diet, while some occur as a result of an overabundance of animal protein or calcium. With a variety of the correct types of food, additional vitamins and minerals, fresh water, and the opportunity to bask in sunlight or artificial sunlight, you should not have problems with such conditions.

The neck of this Green Iguana, *Iguana iguana*, has been badly burned, probably from contact with a heat lamp. Photo by Anthony L. Del Prete

Wounds and Injuries
Wounds and broken bones may be caused by fighting, by attempting to escape, by being crushed by falling objects in the cage, or by burning. Most injuries are preventable. Some wounds may need to be swabbed with a mild veterinary antiseptic such as povidone iodine. Deeper wounds

Abscesses
Soft lumps developing below the skin are abscesses caused by infections entering through a small wound. Untreated, some abscesses can literally eat away the flesh. Abscesses often require veterinary antibiotic treatment and/or surgery.

A pair of ticks. The large one is fully engorged with the host's blood. Photo by Ken Lucas

Ticks and Mites

These arachnid pests are the most common external parasites of lizards. Wild-caught specimens often have ticks attached to them. They should be removed by first dabbing with a little alcohol to loosen their mouthparts, then gently pulling them out of the skin.

Mites can be the bane of the lizard keeper. These tiny, globular parasites are smaller than a pinhead and can proliferate to large numbers in the terrarium before they are even noticed. Numerous mites can cause stress, anemia, dermatitis, and shedding problems. Additionally, the mites can transmit pathogenic organisms from the blood of one lizard to the next. Once a mite infestation has been ascertained, the animals should be treated

A colony of mites living behind the ear of a Crevice Spiny Lizard, *Sceloporus poinsetti*. Photo by Paul Freed

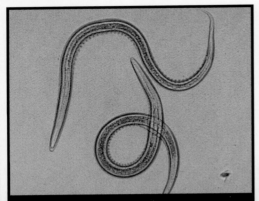

Hookworm larvae found in a *Boa constrictor*. Photo by E. Rundquist

with a suitable chemical available from your pet shop. Terraria should be stripped down and thoroughly disinfected.

Worm Infections

Most wild lizards play host to one or more species of intestinal worms. Under normal conditions the relationship is symbiotic and little harm is done to the host. Under stress, however, worm infestations of the intestine can be dangerous, resulting in compaction, malnutrition, and anemia. To be on the safe side it is advisable to have fecal samples of your lizards checked for worms in a veterinary laboratory. Infestations can be treated with proprietory vermicides available from your veterinarian.

Enteric Infections

Various enteric diseases are caused by a host of bacteria and

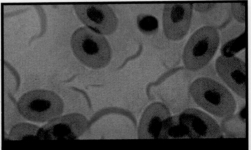

Parasites in the blood of a Timber Rattlesnake, *Crotalus horridus*. Photo by Paul Freed

protozoa. These include salmonellosis (food poisoning), which can be transmitted to humans (all the more reason for sound personal hygiene). Lizards suffering from enteric infections will show signs of lethargy and general debilitation coupled with diarrhea. Such infections require immediate veterinary attention.

An amoebic cyst found in a Water Monitor, *Varanus salvator*. Photo by E. Rundquist

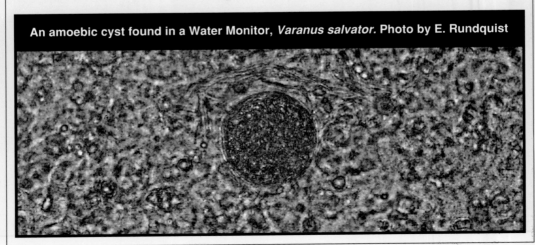

LIZARD PROPAGATION

Due to the increasing reduction in numbers of many lizard species in the wild, it is essential that captive breeding programs should be developed and maintained. Unfortunate as it may seem, it appears that some species may only survive under the protection of captive environments unless more serious conservation measures are taken now. Many lizard species now are regularly bred in captivity, but, in contrast to other kinds of domestic animals, there is still much to be learned about lizard propagation. What we do know is that lizards are unlikely to breed unless they are provided with the kinds of environmental and seasonal conditions prevailing in their native habitats.

Many lizards from temperate and subtropical areas rely on a period of winter hibernation to bring them into breeding condition. It is not necessary for such lizards to complete a full period of hibernation in captivity, and a short "rest period" at cooler temperatures will provide a satisfactory compromise. This can be accomplished by gradually decreasing the temperature and photoperiod in the terrarium over several days while reducing feeding. You should aim to get the temperature down to about 10°C (50°F) for most temperate species or 15°C (59°F) for many subtropical species. It will help if you know something about the climates of your lizards' native habitats. You can get such information from a good geographical atlas. During the cooling period, the lizards will become lethargic and will hide away in their shelters. When you wish to end the compromise hibernation period, which can be anything from two to three months long, you should reverse the procedures described above, gradually bringing the temperature back to optimum over a period of several days and also increasing the photoperiod. As soon as the lizards become active you can begin to feed them again.

COURTSHIP AND MATING

As most lizards live fairly solitary lives for most of the year, it is often best to keep the sexes separate until you wish them to breed. The sudden introduction of a female to a male in his own territory often will initiate a breeding response. In some cases the introduction of two females to two males will further increase the possibilities of mating as the territorial instincts of the males against each other will fool them into mating "before the opponent gets a chance."

Courtship procedures among lizards vary from species to species. A standard courtship sequence is that a sexually

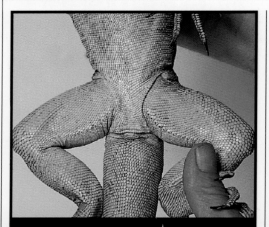

The enlarged pores on the thighs (femoral pores) of this Green Iguana, *Iguana iguana,* indicate that it is a male. Photo by Isabelle Francais.

MALE OR FEMALE?

One very important parameter to breeding success is the possession of a true pair, at least one male and one female. While a very few species have been shown to be able to reproduce without male fertilization (parthenogenetic), the vast majority practice sexual reproduction. Many lizard species show some differences between the sexes. These may include variations in general size, color, shape, tail length, behavior, and so on. In some species the presence or absence of femoral or pre-anal pores will give a clue. As the male hemipenes are inverted into the base of the tail when dormant, this usually means a male has a correspondingly thicker tail base than the female. In some cases the presence of hemipenes can be detected by

aroused male will approach his intended mate and display to her. This may include head bobbing, tail waggling, and bodily contortions all meant to impress the female, which more often than not will appear to ignore his attentions or even run away. After a while the male attempts to grasp the female in his jaws, usually on the neck or upper back. Once subdued, the female will allow him to bend the rear part of his body beneath hers so that their corresponding cloacal regions come into apposition, enabling him to insert one of his erect hemipenes into her cloaca.

Depending on the species, copulation may take anything from a few minutes to several hours. In some cases lizard mating appears rather a violent affair, but this is quite natural and serious injuries rarely occur. Never try to intervene in the procedure or the mating may not be successful.

Everting the hemipenes of a male blue-tongued skink, *Tiliqua* sp. Have an experienced person show you how to do this, as it is possible to injure the animal. Photo by Isabelle Francais.

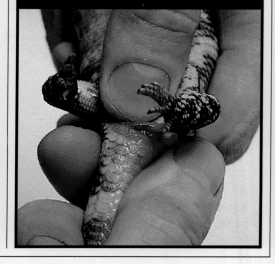

Hatching Rough-Scaled Geckos, *Pachydactylus rugosus.* **Photo by Paul Freed**

squeezing gently at the tail base, causing them to partially evert. Of course, in many lizards squeezing the tail immediately results in autotomy, so perhaps this is not such a wise move after all.

CARE OF EGGS

Once successfully fertilized, eggs will begin to develop in the female. She will become progressively plumper as the eggs increase in size, and eventually you may be able to see and feel the eggs pressing against the sides of her abdomen. The speed at which the eggs develop will depend on species and conditions and may vary from 30 to more than 100 days. Wild lizards seek out suitable spots in which to lay their eggs. Areas that can supply the necessary concealment, warmth, and humidity seem to be the main requirements. Most lizards excavate burrows in soft soil in which to lay their eggs.

Others lay them under rocks, logs, or other ground litter, while most geckos lay their small, hard-shelled eggs in crevices in tree bark.

You must supply your captive lizards with suitable facilities for egg-laying. In the case of geckos, a few pieces of rough tree bark will offer a choice. Other species should be offered a deep container of moist sand in which they may excavate a laying burrow. Some individuals may not be happy with what you have offered and will end up scattering their eggs all over the substrate in apparent frustration. You should keep careful watch at egg-laying time so that you can remove the eggs for artificial incubation. With the exception of the eggs of geckos, eggs left to incubate in the terrarium are rarely successful.

With the exception of the geckos, which lay hard-shelled

Hatching Desert Spiny Lizards, *Sceloporus magister.* **Photo by Ken Lucas.**

eggs, most lizard species lay soft, leathery-shelled eggs. These are designed to absorb moisture from the substrate or incubation medium and actually will fill out, increasing in size and weight as incubation progresses.

I have found vermiculite, an inert, absorbent, granular insulation material, to be by far the best incubation material, but success with sand, peat, or sphagnum moss also is possible. Vermiculite can be mixed with its own weight of water and placed in a plastic incubation box with just a few ventilation holes punched in the lid (it is important to have some air movement without losing too much humidity). The eggs are partially buried in the vermiculite, with about one-third of their surface area exposed to allow regular inspection.

The egg box should be placed in a heated incubator, the interior of which is maintained at 25-30°C (77-86°F). Several makes of suitable incubators are available on the market, but I have successfully used a lidded Styrofoam fruit box partially filled with water. Two bricks are placed in the water so that they break the water surface, and the egg box is placed on top of these. The water is heated with a thermostatically controlled

A juvenile *Riopa fernandi*, an African skink that lives in tropical forests. Photo by R. D. Bartlett

Like many other neonatal lizards, this White-Throated Monitor, *Varanus albigularis* *"ionides,"* will get considerably duller as it grows. Photo by R. D. Bartlett.

aquarium heater. Adjust the heater until the air in the chamber can be maintained at the required temperature. You will require a good thermometer in order to do this. A glass tank or a wooden box could also be used as an incubator, and you have a choice of all kinds of heaters, from lamps to cables, pads to panels. Whatever you use, you must maintain the optimum temperature thermostatically and ensure that humidity remains high around the eggs.

Eggs may take from 30 to 100 days to hatch, again depending on species and conditions. You must inspect the eggs regularly, but do not move them about unnecessarily. You must be especially vigilant as hatching time approaches so that you can remove the babies to nursery housing when they hatch.

LIVEBEARING LIZARDS

Some species give birth to fully formed juveniles rather than lay eggs. Such species are described as ovoviviparous, which means that the embryos develop full term in the mother's body and hatch from their membranous eggs just before, during, or just after deposition. This makes life somewhat easier for the breeder of such lizards as the period of

Here are an adult and a hatchling Fat-tailed Gecko, *Hemitheconyx caudinctus*. Keep baby lizards separate from adults who may eat them. Photo by Paul Freed.

artificial incubation is dispensed with. However, as some adult livebearers have no qualms about adding their own youngsters to the menu, it is best to remove them to separate accommodations as soon as possible after birth.

REARING THE YOUNG

Whether hatched from eggs or live-born, juvenile lizards are best raised separately from the adults in their own cages. Tiny lizards can be housed in small plastic boxes that are stored in a larger heated chamber. Screening is glued over holes in the lids of the plastic boxes to allow for adequate ventilation, plus the admittance of broad-spectrum lighting for those species that require it. You will require a variety of very small insects, such as hatchling crickets or fruitflies, for the tiniest of these reptiles. During the initial period of growth a balanced diet is extremely important. You should shake powdered vitamin/mineral supplement over the food insects about twice per week. Provide the youngsters with a very shallow dish of water that must be changed regularly.

Hatchling Water Dragons, *Physignathus cocincinus*, basking. The dark one is a melanistic individual. Photo by Paul Freed.

SOME SUGGESTED SPECIES

With about 20 families, 350 genera, and over 3000 species, lizards form the largest group of reptiles. In this small introductory work it is possible to include only a token number of all species. The species I have selected to discuss here are those that frequently are available; most also are extensively bred in captivity. I also have included a few of my favorites that may be available occasionally. The lengths given are the maximum head and tail lengths one would expect to find; in many cases the average length is somewhat shorter.

FAMILY GEKKONIDAE—THE GECKOS

With about 800 species and subspecies, this is one of the largest lizard families. Geckos have colonized most parts of the tropics and parts of some temperate regions. Some typical characteristics of geckos are their adhesive toe pads that allow them to run over smooth vertical surfaces and even to move upside-down on ceilings, etc. Most geckos lack movable eyelids and have a transparent spectacle like snakes. Most species are nocturnal. Many geckos make ideal pets for the home terrarium

Impressive coloration and a voracious appetite explain the popularity of the Tokay Gecko, *Gekko gecko.* Photo by Karl H. Switak.

Bibron's Gecko, *Pachydactylus bibroni,* is a very hardy lizard that occasionally has been bred in captivity. Photo by Karl H. Switak

and some frequently are bred in captivity.

Tokay Gecko
Gekko gecko

Length: 35 cm (14 in). One of the largest gecko species, the Tokay is frequently available and is regularly bred in captivity. Being a member of the subfamily Gekkoninae (as are the next three species described), it has the typical main gecko features. Hailing from the jungles of Southeast Asia, this spectacular species has a robust head and body and a relatively slender tail. The color is slaty blue, covered rather evenly with large pink to orange spots. Though they are generally hardy in captivity, Tokay

Frequently available and inexpensive, African House Geckos, *Hemidactylus mabouia,* make great pets for beginners. Photo by R. D. Bartlett.

Geckos have an aggressive and unfriendly disposition and will not hesitate to bite. They are therefore to be admired rather than petted. They are named after their loud "to-keh" call that usually occurs at night. A pair of Tokays should be kept in a tall, semihumid terrarium with dimensions at least 50 x 50 x 90 (20 x 20 x 36 in). Provide several climbing branches. Maintain the temperature at 25-30°C (77-86°F) during the day, reduced to around 20°C (68°F) at night. Tokays are voracious feeders and will take a variety of invertebrates. Large specimens may take pinkie mice.

The beautiful Boehme's Giant Day Gecko, *Phelsuma madagascariensis boehmi*, requires broad-spectrum lighting to stay in good health. Photo by R. D. Bartlett.

Phelsuma lineata, the Lined Day Gecko, is a handsome small day gecko that is occasionally available. The care of this species is similar to that of the Giant Day Gecko. Since it is smaller, it needs smaller insects and can be kept in a smaller terrarium. Photo by A. Norman.

Bibron's Gecko
Pachydactylus bibroni

Length: 18 cm (7 in). This species is extremely hardy in captivity and is available from time to time. A native of southern Africa, it is mainly crepuscular but frequently is active during the day as well as at dusk and dawn. It is an inhabitant of semiarid woodlands where it lives largely on the trunks and branches of trees or among rocks, concealing itself in hollows and beneath bark. It has a compact body, well-developed toe pads, and a relatively short, thick tail. Color varies through various shades of brown, with a sprinkling of raised light and dark scales. It requires a small cage with adequate hiding places (rocks, branches) and a small water dish. It may be fed on a variety of insects and spiders with a regular vitamin/mineral supplement.

House Gecko
Hemidactylus mabouia

Length 20 cm (8 in). Originating in southern Africa, this species has successfully colonized many parts of Central America and eastern South America. It is one of several species in its genus that often are available. In the wild it frequently is found in and around human habitations, where it often is encouraged due to its insectivorous habits. It is a fairly slender gecko with a soft, delicate, almost transparent skin that is scattered with enlarged granular scales. It is gray to gray-brown with faint darker markings. Most *Hemidactylus* species are hardy

terrarium inmates and will live for several years if given the right conditions. Temperature should be maintained around 28°C (82°F) during the day and reduced to 23°C (74°F) at night. A fairly humid atmosphere is essential, so supply a large water bowl and/or mist spray regularly. All species in the genus will feed on a variety of small invertebrates.

Madagascar Giant Day Gecko
Phelsuma madagascariensis

Length: 25 cm (10 in). Probably the largest and most often available of the several species of day gecko, this species occurs on the island of Madagascar, where it is becoming scarcer due to forest clearance. The ground color is leaf-green, which may be uniform or patterned with red or white patches, making them very attractive lizards. They are active during the day and have round pupils, as opposed to the vertical pupils of nocturnal species. They require a tall, humid, planted terrarium with temperatures in the range 25-30°C (77-86°F), reduced a little at night. They may be fed on a variety of insects and nectar. A good supplement to give them is a 50/50 solution of honey in water provided in a small shallow dish; a sugar lump to which a drop of liquid vitamin/mineral supplement has been added also may be licked. As these geckos have high calcium requirements they should be given a separate small dish of crushed cuttlebone so that they can help themselves when the need arises.

Leopard Gecko
Eublepharis macularius

Length: 25 cm (10 in). This is a large, robust species beautifully patterned with black spots and blotches on a brown or yellow background. Juveniles have a totally different pattern of dark and light bands. It is a member of a subfamily of geckos (Eublepharinae) that are atypical in having eyelids and lacking adhesive toe pads. A regular terrarium subject that is captive-bred on a regular basis, this species is easy to obtain. Native to the arid steppes of Afghanistan, Pakistan,and northwestern India, it requires a fairly dry terrarium but should be supplied with a small dish of drinking water. It will do well with daytime temperatures up to 30°C (86°F), reduced to 20°C (68°F) at night. It will feed on a variety of invertebrates and is especially fond of crickets. A simulated hibernation period at reduced temperatures for a few weeks in the winter will induce breeding.

Leopard Geckos, *Eublepharis macularius,* have endearing faces and can be very docile. Photo by Karl W. Switak

FAMILY IGUANIDAE—THE IGUANAS

At one time containing about 60 genera and over 700 species, it seems that the Iguanidae has now been reduced to just eight genera, while the remaining genera have been allocated to several other families. Most members of the "new" Iguanidae are relatively large, robust lizards with spiny crests. They are native to the mainland of North, Central, and South America, the West indies, the Galapagos Islands, and the islands of Fiji and Tonga.

Green Iguana
Iguana iguana

Length: 160 cm (63 in). These must be among the best known and most revered of pet lizards due to their bizarre and attractive appearance, good temperament, and relative ease of keeping. Native to Central America and northern South America, they have threatened status in many areas due to deforestation and collection for the food and pet

This Leopard Gecko has an aberrant yellow coloration. Breeders often select for odd colors and patterns in this species. Photo by R. D. Bartlett, courtesy of B. Brant

The dinosaur of the living room: the Green Iguana, *Iguana iguana*. Photo by Anthony L. Del Prete

trades. Recent attempts at protecting the species in the wild in some areas should help alleviate the problem. The Green Iguana is a robust lizard with a spiny crest extending from the back of the head along the spine and onto the tail. The male possesses a large, leathery dewlap that it can erect during aggression or sexual activity. Adults are a basic gray-green in color with darker bands, sometimes with bluish or rust highlights. Juveniles are a stunning leaf-green up to about a year of age before they begin to develop the more somber adult coloration. A pair of adult Green Iguanas requires a terrarium with a minimum size of 180 cm long x 180 cm high x 90 cm deep

This handsome baby Green Iguana will need a varied diet and broad-spectrum lighting if it is to thrive. Photo by Marian Bacon.

(approx 6 ft x 6 ft x 3 ft). It should be furnished with a large water vessel and strong branches for climbing. Daytime temperatures should be maintained at 25-30°C (77-86°F), reduced a little at night but never less than 18°C (65°F). Juvenile iguanas are partially insectivorous, but become increasingly more herbivorous as they grow. Adults can be fed on a variety of green foods (fruits and vegetables) cut into bite-sized pieces. Tame specimens will try almost everything from steak and kidney pie to peaches and cream, but such items are best kept to a minimum if you don't want your pets to become overweight. Current research indicates that adult Green Iguanas need no animal protein in the diet and young specimens also can do well without it.

Like its relative the Green Iguana, the Chuckwalla, *Sauromalus obesus*, is mostly herbivorous. Photo by Karl H. Switak

Chuckwalla
Sauromalus obesus

Length: 45 cm (18 in). This desert-dwelling iguanid occurs in the southwestern USA and Mexico, where it lives among rocky outcrops. It is a rather portly lizard that likes to hide in rock crevices when disturbed, taking in air and jamming itself into the cavity, making it extremely difficult to remove. The basic color of the Chuckwalla varies depending on its range; it may be uniformly blackish brown to reddish orange with a dark head and shoulders, sometimes with a black banded, white tail. It requires a dry desert terrarium with basking areas to 40°C (104°F) during the day, but reduced dramatically at night to around 20°C (68°F). Provide a small dish of drinking water and some flat rocks arranged to form crevices. Chuckwallas are almost exclusively vegetarian and should be provided with a range of green foods, including dandelion flowers, fruit, and cactus pads if available.

Desert Iguana
Dipsosaurus dorsalis

Length: 40 cm (16 in). This is another desert-dwelling species from the southwestern USA and northern Mexico. It lives in arid scrubland. Though not so portly looking as the Chuckwalla, it is nevertheless a robust lizard. It is a light buff in color with irregular white spots and bars. When basking in full sun it becomes

Desert Iguanas, *Dipsosaurus dorsalis,* require very high temperatures and broad-spectrum lighting. Photo by Ken Lucas

very light colored, appearing almost white. Its terrarium requirements are as described for the Chuckwalla, and hot day basking temperatures are essential. As well as a general vegetarian diet, I have found them to be partial to the young shoots of pungent herbs such as sage and rosemary. Some also will take insects.

Green or Plumed Basilisk
Basiliscus plumifrons

Length: 65 cm (26 in). The four or five species of basilisks have been removed from the Iguanidae to a new family (Corytophanidae). The Plumed Basilisk must be one of the most bizarre looking of all lizards and, as such, is a prize terrarium exhibit. Native to the steamy rain forests of southern Central America, it is a tree-dweller but will not hesitate to take to water if danger threatens, often running so fast on its hind legs over the water surface that it does not sink for several meters. It also can swim very well if the occasion arises. It is a streamlined lizard with long limbs and has a double crest on its head, a high crest along its back, and another along the tail (muuch lower in females than males). The ground color is bright green with bluish spots and highlights (much more subdued in females), with a bright golden yellow eye. Basilisks require a humid, tropical rainforest terrarium with a large water vessel and adequate climbing facilities. Daytime temperatures can rise as high as 30°C (86°F), but reduce to about 24°C (75°F) at night. They feed on a variety of invertebrates; large specimens will take pinkie mice or even small, live freshwater fish.

Helmeted Iguana
Corytophanes cristatus

Length: 35 cm (14 in). Members of this genus have been placed in the newly formed family Corytophanidae along with the basilisks and casque-headed iguanas (*Laemanctus*). *C. cristatus* occurs in the southern parts of Central America, living in the tree canopy, but with less reliance on water than the basilisks. The slender body is laterally compressed. The "helmet" extends as a spiny ridge from the top of each eye and joins at the neck, where the spines continue down the back. The ground color is brown, marked with darker blotches and bands. These lizards should be housed in a humid rainforest terrarium, though only a small, shallow water vessel is required. The temperatures are as described for *Basiliscus*. Feed on a variety of invertebrates.

In appearance, Helmeted Iguanas, *Corytophanes cristatus,* recall the dragons of fantastic stories. Photo by Karl H. Switak

Green Basilisks, *Basiliscus plumifrons,* are beautiful but often high-strung lizards. A large enclosure is necessary. Photo by John C. Murphy

FAMILY AGAMIDAE—THE AGAMIDS

The agamids form the Old World versions of the iguanas, and many species show superficial resemblances to species of iguanas, having crests, dewlaps, and other interesting appendages. The family contains about 35 genera and over 300 species.

Asian Water Dragon
Physignathus cocincinus

Length: 75 cm (30 in). This popular species is being increasingly bred in captivity and should not be too difficult to obtain. Although not closely related, it bears a remarkable resemblance in shape and color to the Green Iguana. Native to Southeast Asia, the Water Dragon lives in wooded areas, usually close to permanent water. The basic color is green, often suffused with pink and blue tones around the throat and flanks. The long, tapering tail is banded with brown. It requires a large terrarium with a voluminous water vessel and stout climbing branches. It likes a daytime temperature up to 30°C (86°F), but this should be reduced at night to around 23°C (74°F). Unlike the Green Iguana, this

Water Dragons, *Physignathus cocincinus,* resemble Green Iguanas but are not closely related to them. Photo by Aaron Norman.

Inland Bearded Dragons, *Pogona vitticeps,* will readily breed if given a short winter cooling. Photo by R. D. Bartlett

species is almost totally carnivorous and should be fed on a variety of larger invertebrates as well as small mice. Some may take a small amount of soft, ripe fruit.

Bearded Dragon
Pogona barbata

Length 45 cm (18 in). Formerly known as *Amphibolurus barbatus*, this species is presently being captive-bred in small numbers. A native of eastern and southeastern Australia, its name arises from the large gular pouch or "beard" that it inflates when alarmed or territorially threatened. It is basically mottled gray and brown in color, paler when the lizard is basking. In the wild it occurs in a variety of habitats from woodland to open scrubland, often in arid areas. It requires a large terrarium with basking temperatures to 40°C (104°F), but should have cooler areas to retire to when necessary; reduce the temperature to room level at night. Broad-spectrum lighting should be provided. The Bearded Dragon will feed on a variety of invertebrates, pinkie mice, and sometimes a little ripe fruit. Provide it with a small dish of water. Over the past few years this species has been largely replaced in captivity by the Interior Bearded Dragon, *Pogona vitticeps*, a somewhat smaller species with a paler throat; it has been bred in very large numbers of late.

Spiny-tailed Agama
Uromastyx acanthinurus

Length: 35 cm (14 in). The bizarre appearance of this species makes it a prized terrarium subject, though it is not as readily available as it was in the past. It has a thick-set, flattened body, a broad head, and a short, thick, spiny tail. When at rest, its body color is dull olive-brown, but when basking it takes on a marbling of yellow and black, with the head almost jet-black. Native to North Africa, it often takes refuge in burrows. It requires a desert terrarium with a deep sandy substrate. Maintain the air temperature at 25-30°C (77-86°F) during day with the basking area to 40°C (104°F). Broad-spectrum lighting is essential. A small dish of water should be available. Almost totally herbivorous, it should be fed on a variety of fruits and vegetables; it may take the occasional mealworm or cricket. Difficult feeders can often be tempted with yellow flowers, especilly dandelions.

Some African Spiny-Tailed Agamas, *Uromastyx acanthinurus,* will eat softened bird seed as a supplement to a varied vegetarian diet. Photo by Isabelle Francais

Leaf litter and soil is a good substrate for a terrarium with a Broad-Headed Skink, *Eumeces laticeps*. Photo by R. D. Bartlett.

FAMILY SCINCIDAE—THE SKINKS

This large family of lizards contains about 50 genera and over 600 species, with representatives on all continents except Antarctica. Most skinks are elongate, circular in cross-section, and have a long tapering tail and short limbs. However, exceptions include species with relatively short tails or with reduced or absent limbs.

Broad-headed Skink
Eumeces laticeps

Length 30 cm (12 in). This, one of the largest US skinks, occurs in the southeastern quarter of the country. It has a robust body and, as its name implies, a broad head. The body color is brown, with five stripes that become fainter with age. The male has a red head. In juveniles, the tail is bright blue, changing to brown with maturity. They live in open woodlands and are partially arboreal, foraging for insects among the foliage of trees and taking refuge beneath bark or in tree hollows. They require a medium sized woodland terrarium with temperatures in the range 21-24°C (70-75°F) plus additional basking facilities. Reduce the temperature at night. Provide a shallow water vessel and feed on a range of invertebrates and pinkie mice.

As the name implies, the Prehensile-tailed Skink, *Corucia zebrata,* has a strong, flexible tail that aids in climbing. Photo by Ken Lucas.

Prehensile-tailed Skink
Corucia zebrata

Length: 60 cm (24 in). This extraordinary skink is now becoming more readily available as the forests of the Solomon Islands come down at an alarming rate. As such it is a by-product of the devastating denudation of the land. If the species is to be saved it will probably be as a result of captive breeding, with which some success has already been achieved. The skink is arboreal and herbivorous, with a strong, prehensile tail. The basic color is olive to brown marked with darker stripes and blotches. It requires a tall, humid rainforest terrarium with facilities to climb. Daytime temperatures can be as high as 30°C (86°F), reduced to about 24°C (75°F) at night. Only a small drinking vessel is necessary. Feed on a variety of greenfood, including fruit and vegetables; it is especially fond of the leaves of large climbing pothos plants. A regular vitamin/mineral supplement is essential.

Eastern Blue-tongued Skink
Tiliqua scincoides

Length: 45 cm (18 in). This attractive, popular, and docile native of Australia is bred fairly regularly and is frequently available, though it may be expensive. It has a rather long, thick body, short limbs, and a broad head. The body color varies from brown to gray with light and dark transverse bars. It requires a large terrarium with a leaf litter or bark substrate and a water vessel in which it may bathe. Provide a

The Prehensile-tailed Skink is also sold under the names Solomon Island Skink and Monkey-Tailed Skink. Photo by Ken Lucas.

The **Common Blue-tongued Skink,** *Tiliqua scincoides,* **makes a hardy and docile pet. Photo by Karl H. Switak**

hiding cave or hollow log and a basking area to 35°C (95°F). Reduce the temperature to around 20°C (68°F) at night. Fairly easy to feed, the Eastern Blue-tongue will take a variety of invertebrates and is especially fond of snails and clean earthworms. It also will take soft fruit such as banana, minced lean beef, and canned cat or dog food.

FAMILY CORDYLIDAE—GIRDLED LIZARDS

So called because of the girdled or belted appearance of the large scales that are reinforced by bony scutes beneath, the family includes two subfamilies: Cordylinae, the typical girdled lizards, and Gerrhosaurinae, the

The **Common Girdled Lizard,** *C. cordylus,* **can be kept in the same conditions as Jones's Armadillo Lizard,** *C. jonesi.* **Photo by R. D. Bartlett**

plated lizards. All are native to Africa and Madagascar.

Jones' Armadillo Lizard
Cordylus jonesi

Length: 15 cm (6 in). Though one of the smaller members of the family, this native of southern Africa is one of the easiest captives. The body and limbs are furnished with large, spiny scales, with similar rings of scales along the tail. The head is triangular, with spines along the back edge. The color is plain brown on the back, whitish beneath. Breeding males may show a reddish tinge on the neck. It requires a

The **Sungazer,** *Cordylus giganteus,* **is impressive but rarely offered for sale. Photo by Karl H. Switak**

semidesert terrarium furnished with rocks and caves. Provide basking temperatures to 35°C (95°F), but ensure there are cooler spots. Reduce the temperature to around 20°C (68°F) at night. Feed on a range of small invertebrates and provide a small water vessel.

Yellow-throated Plated Lizard
Gerrhosaurus flavigularis

Length: 60 cm (24 in). Also native to southern Africa, this species lacks the spines of the

The Giant Plated Lizard, *Gerrhosaurus validus,* consumes a fair amount of vegetation as well as invertebrates. Photo by Karl H. Switak

armadillo lizards, the scales being arranged as squarish plates. If it can be obtained, this species makes an entertaining pet, soon becoming docile and friendly. It is light brown on the back with a pale stripe along each flank. The throat and underside are yellow. Though requiring a larger cage, its climatic requirements are similar to those described for Jones' Armadillo Lizard. It also is more omnivorous and may take soft fruit and canned dog food as well as the more usual invertebrate diet.

FAMILY LACERTIDAE—TYPICAL LIZARDS

With about 200 species in 22 genera, this family forms the "typical" lizards of Europe, Asia, and Africa. All are similar in general shape, with streamlined body, well-developed limbs, and a long, tapering tail.

European Green Lizard
Lacerta viridis

Length 40 cm (16 in). A native of central and southern Europe, this species will do well in captivity if given the right conditions. The male is bright green, developing tinges of blue in the breeding season. Females and youngsters are duller green, sometimes with a series of stripes along the body. It requires a large well-ventilated terrarium with air temperatures about 25°C (77°F) and a hotter basking area. Reduce

This is a young male Green Lizard, *Lacerta viridis.* Although frequently kept in Europe, this species seldom is available in the United States. Photo by R. D. Bartlett.

the temperature at night. It may be kept in an enclosed area outdoors in suitable climates. Feed it on large invertebrates, pinkie mice, and canned cat or dog food.

FAMILY TEIIDAE—TEGUS AND RACERUNNERS

Widely distributed from the USA through Central America to south-central Argentina and Chile, the teiids form a varied family with some 200 species in 40 genera. Many bear a superficial resemblance to lacertids, but there also are a few almost limbless, burrowing species.

Common Tegu
Tupinambis teguexin

Length: 120 cm (48 in). Tegus are perhaps the best known members of the family. The Common Tegu is native to tropical South America, where it occurs in a variety of habitats. This large, aggressive lizard, with its strong bite and sharp claws, is perhaps not suited for beginners, but it is an interesting subject for the more advanced herpetologist. The color is a glossy dark brown to black with numerous golden speckles. Tegus require a large, secure terrarium with firmly anchored furnishings, including a hollow log or hide-box and a large water bath. Maintain daytime temperatures in the region of 30°C (86°F), reduced to not less than 22°C (74°F) at night. Tegus are especially fond of snails, but also will take chicks, mice, lean minced meat, and raw eggs. A vitamin/mineral supplement should be regularly included in the diet.

The Green Lizard consumes earthworms, snails, and fruit along with arthropods and small mammals. Photo by Paul Freed.

Captive-bred Gold Tegus, *Tupinambis teguixin*, tame more easily than wild-caught specimens. Photo by Isabelle Francais.

INDEX

Page numbers in **boldface** refer to illustrations.